THE CHANGING JOB JUNGLE

How to Find Your Almost Perfect Career

"*The Changing Job Jungle* is a creative and compact handbook for every job seeker. Whether they're first-time job hunters or seasoned pros, the book offers simple and strategic suggestions.

"I'm sure millions of people will enjoy reading and employing your different suggestions. And I know they'll be better off if they do.

"In the continual hunt for challenge, fulfillment and success, *The Changing Job Jungle* can help anyone stalk and bag the perfect job."

Rick Kessler
President, AD FACS

"As I read your book, *The Changing Job Jungle: How to Find Your Almost Perfect Career*, I thought many times: "Why didn't I think of that?"

"Your down-to-earth suggestions can be tried, with effectiveness, by anyone.

"Success to you."

Ruth S. Peale
Foundation For Christian Living

"Kurt Kojm...listens and he cares about people and their lifetime quest for a job that is fun and fulfilling."

Arnold "Nick" Carter
Vice President,
Communications Research
Nightingale-Conant Corporation

"There is hope to profit and assimilate in a world where an active industry can be changed drastically overnight with the advent of a new technology."

Laura Pedersen
Author *PLAY $ MONEY*

"Dear Kurt,

"I just finished your book, and can't wait to try to put some of these ideas into action. But not to find a new job. Many of these ideas are transferable to getting a promotion in my current company!

"The book is chock-full of ideas that are applicable to any job and any field. A little thought, and you can use any one of the ideas presented here to make yourself stand out and be noticed, which is the major task of anyone competing for a job."

Lawrence Stachniak
Engineer

"This is not just another job-changing book, but an insightful and practical guide to personal development and achievement that I believe would be invaluable to a college student preparing for the real world."

Thomas W. Mateczun
President
Performance Development Systems

"A complete guide to who you are and where you're going. Don't leave home without it!"

Paul L. Stanley
Research Scientist

"Thanks for sharing *The Changing Job Jungle: How to Find Your Almost Perfect Career.* I enjoyed browsing through it and found it full of common-sense advice for getting the job or just getting ahead. I liked the format and style."

Art Hatton
Vice President for College
Relations and Development,
State University of New York
at Geneseo

"I just finished reading *The Changing Job Jungle: How to Find Your Almost Perfect Career.* I found it very enjoyable. It was uplifting, refreshing and thorough. After putting the book down, I started to dream about all the ways I could use these ideas to enhance my current responsibilities. Your book is a tool box no serious job seeker could do without. It's a must for anyone serious about maximizing their fullest employment potential."

Michael J. Rizzolo
Ultimate Achievement Systems

"From the sensible to the outrageous, Kurt Kojm's *The Changing Job Jungle* will stimulate your creative thinking. Strategic job searching takes on a new excitement. Full of new ideas—and old ideas in new clothing."

Roger E. Herman, CSP, CMC
Author, *Keeping Good People*

"Kurt Kojm wastes no time in getting to his subject in *The Changing Job Jungle.* Starting from page one, this book is packed with useful ideas for anyone contemplating a job or career change. You will want to read this book with a highlighter handy. There are plenty of ideas you will want to put to use. This book can also be useful to consultants and salespeople looking for business-building ideas."

Mitchell R. Alegre and Associates
Products and Services for
Personal and Organizational
Effectiveness

"In a world of vast economic change with so many job-seekers' cure-alls already on the market, the challenge today is to give people just what they need in a form they can use. For that reason, I like Kojm's approach in *The Changing Job Jungle.* Drawing on his substantial personal experience and multiple other self-help sources, he furnishes the career-builder with over 70 techniques and affirmations. His recommendations are laced with empathy and served in bite-size, digestible tidbits—well-suited to the way we learn. For that reason, when mixed with commitment and common sense, I believe Kojm's approach will lead to the actions and self-confidence which are the basis of career success."

Richard W. Morris, Ph.D.
Technology Consultant

"Kurt can help you discover the job you really want. And develop a successful game plan to enjoy it. For your best-ever performance!"

Dr. Philip Johnson
Life & Leadership Coach of
"Champions"

"Kurt Kojm's strategies for job seekers and for life are realistic, creative and-energy driven. *The Changing Job Jungle* is a terrific book."

James Rolek
Director of Personnel

"A thoroughly enjoyable read, with very imaginative and creative tips for distinguishing a job candidate from the competition."

Andrea Thomas, Attorney

"Besides being a how-to book, it also serves as a real self-esteem booster. Feeling inadequate? Read this book to find out all the things you are really capable of doing and being."

Lucille C. Stanley
Business Owner, REMOS

"The complete survival kit for the hunter on job safari."

Dennis Lelek
Manager, Accounts Payable

"Kurt's new book provides a wealth of strategies for marketing yourself to potential employers. His ideas are unique, creative and are sure to grab the attention you need to stand out from the crowd. A worthwhile tool for any job seeker."

Randy Straight
Territory Manager

"Get this book. Read Kurt's book! It's a goldmine of valuable information that will get you on the road to your perfect job."

Joe Sabah
Co-author of *How to Get the Job You Really Want and Get Employers to Call You*

THE CHANGING JOB JUNGLE

How to Find Your Almost Perfect Career

BY KURT BARNABY KOJM

FOREWORD BY
Jerrold H. Nowacki

About Face Press
Buffalo, New York

Permissions Department
About Face Press
1833 Kensington Avenue, Buffalo, NY 14215. (716) 862-9530

Printed in the United States of America

Edited by Catherine A. Kennedy
Cover Photo by Jim Bush
Graphic Design by Bob Rosenberry
Printed by Partners' Press Inc.

ISBN 1-879799-00-6

DEDICATION

1st To my best friend, my wife Joanne. Her patience, fortitude and love kept this project on course.

2nd To my team of advisors that shared their views and comments.

3rd To the thousands of people that have benefitted from the ideas in the book and have made them their reality.

FOREWORD

When my friend, Kurt Kojm, asked me to contribute some thoughts to *The Changing Job Jungle,* I was flattered and I asked him, "why me?" Kojm said, "Because you are street-smart and the book has non-traditional ideas you'll like." I took home the final draft and couldn't put it down. WOW, finally a compilation of bottom-line strategies to give you ideas, insights, motivation and reasons to want to succeed. Not only is this book excellent for the novice or executive career searcher, but here is a book senior management in Corporate America should read. People are constantly on the lookout for better jobs. They compete for positions and hope they get selected. Here is your chance to develop and utilize strategies that will catapult you past the competition. Today the well-rounded individual looks at a career as a labor of love. He invests the time now to help guarantee the future. Here's your chance to simplify your Changing Job Jungle. If you're a novice or corporate executive looking for fresh, invigorating information, stop here. The journey begins inside.

Jerrold A. Nowacki
Chief Executive Officer
Progressive Direct Marketing

TABLE OF CONTENTS

SECTION IV

How to Get Hired

SECTION V

Interviewing

SECTION VI

The Follow-Up

SECTION VII

Standing Out

SECTION VIII

Special Interest Groups

SECTION IX
Conclusion

INTRODUCTION

Welcome to the Game of Life... and congratulations on picking up this survival guide. You've just changed your life by taking the first step toward improvement. Whether your goal is a new job, more clients, or better people skills, the suggestions in this book will help you attain it.

Think of me as your coach in this game — my real purpose in writing this book is to share my exciting strategies with you; teach you how to practice, practice, practice; and then finally make you a winner!

The World University Games will be held in my home town — Buffalo, New York. This is the first time EVER that a U.S. city has hosted this event, and there are 7,000 athletes and officials from 120 countries participating. Eighty percent of these outstanding athletes are also Olympians. What was it that took these 7,000 people to the *top* of their field? CONFIDENCE, coupled with talents that they were able to recognize and finely tune.

What we do at About-Face Executive Marketing Services, and what this book will do, is to help YOU discover those hidden talents, and show you how to fine tune them. Our goal is to help people grow, define their goals, and map out strategies to achieve them. We then provide the motivation to go after those dreams!

We "recycle" people — by learning about their existing skills and talents, we show people how they are actually suited to a number of different employment opportunities. You're more qualified than you might think for that "perfect" job!

You can always be a better person today than you were yesterday, and better still tomorrow than you are today.

Today's world is changing dramatically. Corporations are downsizing, merging, separating, growing, and then beginning the cycle all over again. How can you survive in this jungle of change? The key is flexibility — positioning yourself as adaptable, capable, and willing to work hard in a new situation.

Here is the best tool on the market — come learn what it takes to be a WINNER!

SECTION I

FOLLOW YOUR DREAMS

STRATEGY 1

The Trail to Success

What do you really want out of life? If you could do anything, what would it be? Did you know that there's a reason you picked up this book? Nothing is accidental!

All journies, large or small, begin the same way — inch by inch, step by step, one day at a time. I'm going to introduce you to a four-step process that will help you to reach those goals that you've only dreamed of until today.

Step One -
Unleash Your Dreams — After Thinking Them Through
Step Two -
Write Them Down — Give Life to Your Thoughts
Step Three -
Visualization — When You Believe It, You'll See It
Step Four -
Accept the Destiny You've Created for Yourself

These steps will be detailed in the next few chapters — it's important that you understand the whole process, and follow the course in its entirety. This program will work in virtually any aspect of your life — career, education, relationships, or any goal you've always wanted to achieve.

STRATEGY 2

Dream Away

The new house...the red sports car...the perfect job...when you daydream, what do you imagine yourself doing? Remember back to when you were in the first grade — what did you want to be when you "grew up?"

My point is that you have to recognize and define those dreams, turn the images into ideas, and let those ideas set you free. Everything that now exists began as someone's thought — every building, book, and broomstick. All you need to do is add action, and you've created a reality from that simple dream.

STRATEGY 3

Do It – WRITE!

Here's how we crystallize our thinking — write down your ultimate goals. List 50 things you enjoy doing right now (both on and off the job), and start thinking about how to incorporate them into your everyday life. (Incidentally, they will also help us to pick up great job skills, but that's another chapter!)

You may see pictures in magazines of where you'd like to go, what you'd like to do, who you'd like to look like — cut them out! Create a "dreamboard" that you can use every day to remind yourself of where your life is heading.

There's something about putting the pen to paper that can turn a fantasy into reality — you've taken a dream and turned it into a GOAL.

Stay with us on this idea of thoughts fueling the power of the pen. Remember that all thought is creative, and that it's your thinking that has brought you this far in life (whether it's positive OR negative!). Adjusting your cerebral focus will change your entire life!

STRATEGY 4
Snapshots of the Perfect Jungle

Visualization is a successful technique that's used by many of today's leaders. Once your objectives are defined on paper, go to the next step and picture yourself doing the things you've always wanted to do, and living the way you've always dreamed of living.

Using this technique is different from daydreaming — with visualization, you actually *consciously* see yourself in the situation you desire. You've got the office in the corner with the big window — which way would your desk face?...that summer house on the bay — where would you go fishing?...working with that big client — what kind of projects would you tackle? By dealing with these situations, you give yourself the confidence and the motivation to search for ways to make them actually happen.

Take 15 or 20 minutes of "quiet time" every morning to visualize your new surroundings, even if it means getting up a little earlier. This is *mental* exercise, it will refresh you and give you a positive attitude in the same way that physical exercise provides energy.

Replace worry and procrastination (life's two biggest time-wasters) with desire and *action* — and watch the results! Remember that your attitude is the fundamental reason for succeeding or failing; anything is as easy as you make it. Add a little effort, and you'll be amazed at how you can turn your life around.

STRATEGY 5

Accept Your Destiny

You *can* create *your own* luck — and when opportunity knocks, you can accept it with open arms.

Too many people are afraid to take chances, they stick with the same old routine day after day until it becomes as comfortable as an old shoe. Just remember this powerful thought from Earl Nightingale: ***"a rut is nothing more than a grave with the ends kicked out."***

Be willing to accept challenges, and to take risks with your career, your relationship, your whole life. Life doesn't have any time-outs; everything counts either toward your pleasure of living or shrinking to the pain of limiting your God-given ability. Which do you really want?

Break Time

Take some time to absorb what you just learned.

STOP

Go outside for some fresh air.
When you return let's see what's on your lists.

Check out the career skills list on page 95. How does it compare with your inventory?

SECTION II

Plant the Seeds and Watch Your Self-Confidence Grow

STRATEGY 6

Chart Your Path So Far

Look at how far you've come in the world — to help you build self-confidence, I want to know about your accomplishments from day one. A common technique that you'll notice throughout the book is to put your thoughts into writing. Take 10 minutes out here and list every award you've won, every promotion you've earned, and every good deed you've performed since birth!

From winning the spelling bee in first grade to receiving a Nobel prize, include everything. Once this list is finished, you'll be amazed at your own strengths and their value to others. Keep this document in a prominent place, where you'll see it every day. This will help you to affirm your belief in yourself, and at the same time encourage you to add to your list of achievements.

P.S. You've already won the race by becoming involved with the planning process!

STRATEGY 7
Mirror Yourself

Another self-confidence building technique is "mirror work." Set up a mirror, enlist a friend's help, and watch your facial expressions as you go through a presentation, a job interview, or a discussion about your relationship. Body language is very powerful — look for eye contact, posture, gestures.

Work on reflecting the mood of the person who's interviewing you — when he's relaxed, you should be, too. If he's intent on making a point or asking a question, you should be leaning forward, expressing interest and building a rapport with him.

Things like direct eye contact are important, they open people up and help them to trust you. What is your first impression of someone who never looks you right in the eye? Shy, nervous, dishonest? By using a mirror, you can put yourself in the client's shoes for a moment, and see the picture of you that you're presenting. Is it accurate or does it need work?

Finally, smiling is probably the most important body language sign. People like to be near others who make them feel good. If you're open and friendly, smiling gives you the image of a person with high self-esteem and a positive attitude — someone who this potential client/employer/friend will want to get to know better.

STRATEGY 8
Call of the Wild

At this point, I've been inspired to share some of my strategies for the game we call life!

Use motivational books and tapes to get you going every day — send them to friends, family, and potential employers/clients. Call everyone you can and let them know that you enjoy life, and you'd like to share it with them. Inspiring others is a great way to motivate yourself at the same time.

Praying is also a strong motivator for some people — call upon God to help you create and follow your life's plan. The answers are already there, we just have to search for them. Ask for help and something wonderful will happen.

Do you believe in electricity? Has anyone ever seen it, tasted it, smelled it? We see the results of energy every day in labor-saving machines. Faith is the same thing — you don't see it physically, yet there is something there that's producing results. I used an act of faith to write this book. What would I say? Who would read it? YOU ARE. Why do you think that is?

STRATEGY 9
Learn More About the Jungle

Take a course at a local college or high school in a subject you've always wanted to know about. It could be cooking, botany, or philosophy — it doesn't have to be related to your employment to improve your skills. Your abilities grow stronger while you're improving yourself, and learning something new every day is a fantastic way to do just that.

Workshops and seminars are also great ways to keep up-to-date on events in your fields of interest. National conferences are superb ways of putting your finger on the pulse of today's society!

STRATEGY 10

Time to Decide Which Trail to Take

Making good use of your time is the best way to feel productive, and enhance your self-esteem. One common thread for all mankind is time — we have 168 hours each week, 24 hours each day. At a rate of 86,400 seconds per day, how can we ever say "I don't have time"? What we mean is that we must prioritize our needs and put the plan into action.

As Robert Townsend suggested, you must ask yourself, "Is it what I'm doing or about to do getting me closer to our objectives?" If you want a house with a picket fence and you're just wasting time now, you could be about to embark on a new project. If you've got a job you love, but are considering leaving for monetary reasons, consider your long-term goals. Is there another solution to the problem?

Claim your time — don't let time claim you. Keep a daytimer, make it the source of all your information: appointments, contacts, notes from meetings, birthdays, favorite restaurants, etc. It helps to cut through the clutter, and makes you a more organized, effective individual.

You could start each day with a list of priorities, and cross them off as they're completed. This will give you the momentum you need to finish all of the tasks. And when they're done, reward yourself for your improved time management skills — whether it's a half hour in the tub or a call to a favorite friend, remember to be good to yourself.

STRATEGY 11
Putting Off Procrastination

Are you moving closer to what you want, or you are moving away from your destination? Procrastination can prevent even the most highly motivated people from achieving their objectives. The key is to find the reason behind the procrastination — there are five basic fears that fuel this common problem:

Fear of failure	a perfectionist who is critical of himself knows that by not beginning a project, he cannot fail.
Fear of success	someone who perceives danger in being assertive and competitive.
Fear of losing control	he thinks he may end up being dominated and lose his self-worth if he joins in a project.
Fear of separation	he may be afraid of independence and being responsible for himself, so he refuses to grow up, get a job, or end a relationship.
Fear of attachment	he is uncomfortable with closeness and will do anything to avoid a commitment, whether it's to a person, a project, or an employment situation.

Breaking this cycle requires that you identify where the problem lies, and then work slowly but surely to correct it. You may want to keep a time diary for a week or so to pinpoint your weak periods. **Any habit can be transformed in 21 days** by practicing stress reduction techniques when you feel fear coming on. Work with it every day in little ways.

Learn to make decisions quickly and follow through — most of the time, there are no right and wrong decisions. There are just choices! The sooner you make the choice and begin to work on the project, the better the end result. Don't waste time on "should have" and "if only" — learning from your mistakes is all that's really important. Be gentle on yourself.

You can also use small bits of time for easier tasks, and plan to do larger ones in small increments. You already know what stimulates you — focus on the positive and just GO! Usually, once you begin an unpleasant chore, the law of inertia will take over and your body will stay in motion until that chore is DONE!

STRATEGY 12

Leave the Boogles in the Quicksand

What do you do when the "boogles" hit? Those nasty, nagging self-doubts — "Do I have what it takes?", "I have to pay these bills", "I'm not good enough." There are three ways to deal with these everyday worries:

1. *Use affirmations* — positive statements about yourself: "I did a great job on that project", "I'm smart", and "I like myself." By repeating these over and over, you'll foster a strong belief in yourself and replace negative feelings with truly positive ones.

2. *Try a Ben Franklin T-graph* — take a blank piece of paper, and draw a giant "T." Now, on one side of the graph, list all of the positive things going on in your life, all of the pluses. On the other side, list the negatives. By clarifying your thinking (again, employing the writing technique), you'll come up with the right answer, and defeat the "boogles."

3. *Sing* — the final way to fight these evil creatures is simply to sing. Yes, sing. If a positive thought is in your head, it is very difficult for the brain to entertain a negative one at the same time. It <u>is</u> merely a distracting technique, but if you're working on your attitude every day, this is a great way to get rid of a temporary case of "boogles."

SECTION III

NETWORKING

STRATEGY 13

Don't Talk to Strangers

The best way to get in any door is to look at it from the side of the person who'll open it. Future employers or clients will talk to you for four reasons only:

1. **to create wealth — you will make money for them;**
2. **to manage resources — you can save money for them;**
3. **to build rapport — they like you;**
4. **to finish projects —you get things done.**

No one ever hires a stranger. So what you need to do is to start building up your networking skills, and there are a number of ways to do this. The best exercise is to sit down and write out the people you know who could help you or refer you for future employment. Creating this list will give you ideas and form the basis for your network. This basis will lead to "chains of influence" or "chains of referral."

How would you network to the Pope? It's easy. You would speak to your local parish priest, who would send you to the bishop, who in turn would send you to a cardinal, then eventually to the Pope himself. It's the same for the president of IBM—go through a local sales representative to the division manager to a vice president, then to the president. To get to the President of the United States, you can go through the House of Representatives or the Senate — there are always links in the chain that are available locally, and they will help you reach the top.

STRATEGY 14

Let Your Fingers Do the Walking - to the Competition

A great resource is the phone book. You can browse through it, look at headlines, and study the companies you may be interested in contacting. There may be alternate reference headings, so check all of them. If you're presently interviewing or canvassing a corporation, you can use this source to gather information on their competition — how many of this type of business are in the area, are there outside (non-local) firms mentioned, etc. With a few phone calls, you can get a feel for the size of these companies, and perhaps even the demand side of the local market. All of this background will help you to speak knowledgeably when you do meet your prospect (or prospective employer), demonstrating your interest in their business, your preparation skills, and your enthusiasm for working with them.

Trade magazines and conventions or seminars are also excellent sources of this type of information. The workshop angle also gives you a chance to network with important people, and start building the chain we talked about in the previous chapter. This detective work is not easy, but it is rewarding — every hour you put in can mean *thousands* of dollars in revenue once you break into the system.

STRATEGY 15

A Blast From the Past

A fantastic source for building a network is your college or high school yearbook. Contact these people — find out what they're doing. See where their careers are heading, and then ask them who they might know who could help with your job search. (For example, a question like "Who is your electronics supplier?" may lead to an appointment at an engineering firm.)

You can follow up with the alumni office to find out who's doing what from the class of ??.

STRATEGY 16

Book 'Em

A good place to continue your network construction is the public library. The directories, trade magazines, career journals, yearbooks, and local company information are all at your fingertips. You should certainly befriend the librarian — this person can open any door in the library, in the shortest amount of time and most efficient way possible. They can show you how to use all of the resources available, and keep you from wasting valuable time on your search for answers.

These places can also help when developing a mailing list for prospects. The most current information is here — and it's especially useful when you are looking for the M-A-N (person with the Money, Authority, and Need) to contact at a company, whether they're male or female!

STRATEGY 17
Where to Find It

Holy Rollers

Visit the church that the prospective client or boss attends. If they see you at different levels, the probability of your being accepted is greatly increased because you're already a member of their team. They know that you're trying hard to build rapport, and that you have similar interests. As we've said before, people hire people that they like.

P.S. - you may even enjoy the service!

Volunteering: A Win-Win Situation

Getting involved with volunteer work may be the best way to network with community leaders. You'll meet people from all walks of life, in all types of occupations, and they'll help you once you're a friend. Volunteering also looks great on a resume — it testifies to your community spirit and willingness to get involved with projects. Let a company know that you're active in their favorite charity, and that you think this cause is important also.

Associate With the Pros

Join professional or civic associations in fields of interest that you share with potential clients. Reach outside your discipline for new ideas and values. Just because it's not in your field doesn't mean that it's not worthy of partaking. Stretch yourself. Look for an idea outside your normal sphere of influence.

Put on Your Walking Shoes

Travel to workshops or seminars that are related to your profession. National conferences have an added value of contacts and information on a higher level than local ones.

Speaking of Networking

If there's a local speakers bureau, investigate it. Find out who these people are talking to, and what they're talking about. This can present a lot of opportunities for both self-learning and picking up leads on jobs or clients. From CPAs to farmers, there are lecturers on just about every topic. Make yourself an expert, and join the ranks. It's a great vehicle for self-promotion, and for getting the community recognition that will send your career (and self-confidence) sailing.

A Fly-By-Day Operation

Travel first class — find out why people pay more for deplaning 15 seconds earlier.

Be an Athletic Supporter

If it's possible, join the company sports team, or at least the league that they play in. You can sit on the bench, and find out all sorts of information on the company that you'd never hear within the walls of the building. Ask about the new people, the person's boss, how they were hired, what projects are currently being developed, and where they may need help. Becoming a member of the sports team is a great infiltration technique, and the rewards are priceless.

STRATEGY 18

Ask For It

When you make the contact, you must talk value to the potential "buyer." Don't just ask to send your resume, and if they ask you to do that, say "I certainly will, but I also have a couple of ideas that I'd like to share with you. Can we get together next week sometime to discuss these ideas as well as my qualifications?" You must request the order right away — in the form of the meeting, the "big event."

Remind the *M-A-N* (the person with money, authority and need) that you only need a short period of time to get your points across. Be creative when making the appointment, instead of asking for 10 minutes, use an oddball number — "I'm looking at 300 seconds of your time, how about 4:05 on Tuesday?"

Sometimes breakfast meetings are your best bet — the early bird gets the up-and-coming executive. Breakfasts are wonderful for power meetings: the prospect is fresh, alert, and uninterrupted by the office traffic. The few dollars you spend on breakfast will be returned a thousandfold when you make a hit with this individual.

Just remember, when you ask for the appointment, no matter what the time, be direct, be flexible, and make it easy for the person to say "YES."

STRATEGY 19

The Secret of Confirming Appointments

When you do get the interview via the telephone, stand out from the rest of the crowd by using a thank-you card *before* the appointment. A tremendously successful strategy is to write out a simple card: "Thank you for your time and consideration. I know that your time is valuable, and mine is, too. I'm looking forward to seeing you May 18th at 7:33 am. Sincerely, Kurt Kojm."

It should be short and simple — to the point. Mail it to them so that they receive it the day before the appointment. It's a sure-fire way to attract attention and peak interest in you and your product.

Here's another little-known secret for job hunters: research found in the Rizman Report has shown that the last person interviewed for a position gets the job **56%** of the time! The one who interviews first is only hired **14%** of the time. If you think you're among the first few candidates scheduled for appointments, subtly ask to change to a later date. (By the way, as with any appointment, Mondays are usually not good, and mornings are better than afternoons!)

STRATEGY 20

Do You Hear What I Hear?

Practice "active listening" when you go into an appointment. A good technique is to take notes, either written or with a tape recorder. Always get permission from the other person, and 99 times out of 100, they'll say "yes." These notes will help you with the follow-up later on, and will emphasize that you feel this meeting is important and is a valuable source of information.

You should match energies with the other person: if they're aggressive, be a little aggressive; if they're passive, be a little passive.

The most important thing you can do is ask questions. These should have been prepared beforehand, but also refer back to what has already been said. This way, they know that you are paying attention, and that their words are worthwhile. You will appear to be a sharp individual who could be a vital member of their active team.

STRATEGY 21

Mops, Brooms, and Tomatoes

When a salesperson comes to you and says, "I'm selling mops, brooms, and tomatoes," and you don't happen to need any of these things at the moment, that's the end of the story. He's gone. But perhaps you wanted a cucumber, and he was going to have them next week, or you might need brooms next month.

He never established a connection with you — he doesn't know what your needs are, and he just missed a good potential client. The point here is that you should find out what the prospective employer is looking for, and match your skills to that description. You may have experience that is not clearly displayed on your resume, and you'll want to tell him that.

Use the ***6 "W"s***, the ***"I"*** and the ***"H."*** Find out the **what, who,**

where, when, why, which, if, and **how** of the corporation by asking open-ended questions such as: "What are your goals for the next quarter? How are we going to achieve that?" Notice the word "we" worked in to build rapport with the employer. This avoids the "You" and "Me" trap — you're not in opposite camps, you're members of the same team. Emphasize your transferable skills, and maintain the focus on your ability to help that person.

STRATEGY 22

Your Best Friend

The receptionist/secretary is the gatekeeper, and she can sometimes hold the key to your future! Prior to an appointment, you should learn all you can about the company. This is not always easy, so I recommend arriving a little early, and talking to the receptionist.

It's important to treat a receptionist with as much respect as anyone else in the organization. Find out her name, and use it. Chances are, her boss will ask "What did you think of Mr. Jones?" And if she thinks you're a friendly, outgoing person, that's going to help you. If she got the impression that you're a cold, conceited introvert, that's surely not going to work in your favor.

The receptionist is also a goldmine of information. She knows everyone in the company, the personalities and the politics, so she's a good player to have on your side. Directories are fine, but they're not always current — the receptionist knows who's doing what every day.

STRATEGY 23
Building Rapport

Find out what the potential employer's favorite book or film is, and quote from it either during the interview, or in your follow-up procedure. Convince this person that you're interested in their likes and dislikes, and that you have similar tastes.

Volunteer to take on a task for this person — if there's something he or she really hates doing, offer to do it for them. I'm not talking about washing their car or cleaning their garage, but maybe something like making follow-up calls, doing correspondence, anything that might be considered a project. If he sees what you're capable of doing, you have a much greater chance of getting hired or taking him on as a client.

By becoming a helper before you're even working for him, you're learning to work smarter, not harder. You'll also demonstrate your strengths, and discover how you can be an even more valuable asset to the company in the future.

You might find a case and model project from the *Harvard Business School* and adapt it to your employer's situation. Regardless of the position, you're being hired to solve problems for the company, so establish your capabilities right away. Use something that was discussed in your initial interview, find a source, develop a model, and make your presentation!

Brainstorm with other people for new ways of looking at old problems. If you're concerned about something, get a couple of friends together, and look at the challenge from other points of view—you'll be amazed at the solutions they'll come up with. Set a minimum of 35 new ideas, so you'll have a goal to work toward, reach, and surpass.

For that extra-mile project, go beyond the local area for help. Find a specialist. Detail your problem in writing, and ask them to let you know how they would handle this challenge. Then forward that response to your future employer.

STRATEGY 24
Belly Up to the Bar

What happens at quitting time on Friday evening? The married people generally drive home. The unattached folks are usually looking for some excitement. Where do they go? Watch the migration pattern. Follow the automobiles as they head to their favorite watering hole. Go there. Mingle with the players. Settle yourself in with a non-alcoholic beverage and listen to the working drama unfold. Make a few friends and ask, "How can I get a foot in the door?" Before you know it, you will become part of the "gang".

If this sounds a little pushy, back off and bring a friend. Approach the happy hour from a tag team perspective. Sometimes it's easier to talk with strangers through a friend's help. Here's an opportunity to practice your open-ended questions. What department do you work in? How busy is your company? What new products are you developing?

Sit back and actively listen to the response. Surprise! You may be introduced to your next boss. Listen, mingle, and follow up with appropriate material.

STRATEGY 25

105 Different Ways to Network for Your Job

Your mind is all-powerful. Meet and exceed your challenge by exercising the creative thought process. For the next 20 minutes read the list of possible plans to build your network. Keep your eyes and ears attuned to opportunities. The networking process is everywhere. Look in the yellow pages. Scan the newspaper. Attend social functions.

Ask yourself the following questions: Who can I meet that will bring me closer to my goal? What are the products or services? Who are their customers? How can I create wealth for these organizations? How can I save these companies' resources? What projects can I help them complete?

1. Associations listed in the yellow pages section of the phone book.

2. Contact the active political parties.

3. Secure the major events calendar from the convention and visitors bureau.

4. The County Fair - seek out new vendors.

5. Wedding Planners - uncover the supplier's network.

6. Dances/Socials - Where do the participants work?

7. Road Rallies - Expensive cars and fast fuel.
   How do you get involved?

8. Book Signings - Meet who's new and hot in literature and business.

9. Theater/Plays - Who supports the fine arts in the playbill?

10. Celebrity Movie Openings - Rub shoulders with the local rich and famous.

11. Radio Station Remote Broadcasts - Discover the power of the spoken word.

12. Ice Cream Socials - Find out who has a sweet tooth.

13. October Festivals - Mingle with people that love their brew.

14. Church Picnics - Network with parishoners.

15. Ground-Breaking Ceremonies - Uncover buried business.

16. Bicycle Clubs - Connections.

17. Marathon Races - Check sponsorships.

18. Special Olympics - Raise your social consciousness.

19. Day Care Centers - Meet the newly arrived and their parents

20. Scout-O-Ramas - The next generation of leaders.

21. Ice Shows

22 Hockey Games
23. Baseball Games
24. Basketball Games
25. Football Games
26. Soccer Games
27. Lacrosse

What organization would benefit from being associated with a sports team?

28. Seminars/Workshops - Who's interested in self-improvement?

29. Quick Copy Shops - Every small business needs copies.

30. Print Companies - Established organizations gather here for their printed materials.

31. Tanning Salons
32. Health Clubs
33. Counseling Centers
34. Weight Training
35. Weight Reduction Clinics
36. Dance Studios

What organizations are interested in reducing medical liabilities? What firms believe in staying trim?

37. Ski Resorts

38. Golf Courses/Country Clubs

39. Art Museums
40. Science Museums
41. Historical Museums

What companies support the fine arts?

42. Mass Transit Stations - Who do you know in the daily commute?

43. Rock Concerts - Sponsors? Fun-loving people.

44. Post Offices
45. Motor Vehicle Bureaus
46. Government Agencies
47. Supermarkets

Who can you meet in line?

48. Hospitals

49. Volunteer Fire Departments

50. National Guard Meetings

51. Cable TV Consumer Affairs - Watchdogs for better television.

52. Department of Labor
53. County
54. State
55. Federal

Check out the governmental listings in the phone book.

56. Local Municipalities

57. Barber Shops
58. Beauty Parlors/Hair Design

What's the buzz? Excellent sources of information.

59. Rental Centers

60. Beverage Distribution Centers
61. Caterers

Who's active in serving people?

62. Club section of the yellow pages.

63. Computer Stores - What's the latest development?

64. Contractors - What is being built?
65. Trade Shows/Convention Centers
66. Auto Show
67. Home and Garden Shows
68. Recreational Vehicle Shows
69. Business and Computer Shows

Ask who would attend? What sort of vendor will I meet by attending?

70. Piano and Organ Dealers

71. Florists

72. Machine Companies - What do they manufacture?

73. Auto Dealers - Who's buying?

74. Auto Parts Stores - What are the hot aftermarket products?

75. Sound Equipment Vendors

76. Heating, Ventilating and Air Conditioning Contractors

77. Dog Groomers

78. Temporary Placement Services

79. Full Time Placement Counselors

80. Electricians

81. Hardwood Floor Installers

82. Bankers

83. Insurance Agents

84. Brokers

85. Real Estate Developers

86. Building and Grounds Superintendents

87. Importers

88. Exporters

89. Teachers/Instructors

90. Philharmonic
91. Hobby Shops

91. Hobby Shops

92. Horse Dealers

93. Labor Organizations - Huge section in yellow pages.

94. Moving Companies - Who's expanding?

95. Limousine Services

96. Commercial Photographers

97. Graphic Designers

98. Sign Companies - New companies, new energy.

99. Social Service/Welfare Organizations - Listed in plan book.

100. Travel Agencies

101. Truck Sales

102. Audio/Video Production Facilities

103. Freight Forwarders

104. Newspaper Editorials

105. Delivery People - Especially in a repeat business such as printing.

STRATEGY 26

Touchy Techniques to Grab that Interview

You can try some of the following strategies if you think that your prospect is going to be receptive. My feeling is that when you're on the outside looking in, you have nothing to lose, so go ahead and give it a shot!

Recruit people who will call the employer on your behalf. Make connections in your network, and have some contacts make "testimonial calls" for you.

Send your prospect tickets to a ballgame, a play, the theater, anything he or she may be interested in. Or send one ticket, and keep the other so that you'll be seated together, then present your ideas (and yourself) in a more casual atmosphere.

Celebrate the CEO's birthday with a splash, and publicize it by contacting the local media, listing his or her name in the paper, or some other exciting tactic.

Edible gimmicks are great attention-getters: send the manager a cookie with a note - *"You're Hiring A Smart Cookie"* or send candy and say *"I've Got A Sweet Deal For You."* It may be corny, but it **WORKS!**

There are a number of ideas that we've outlined in the follow-up section of this book which certainly could be appropriate for using as initial attention-getters!

If nothing else comes from these techniques, you're generating interest in yourself and your creativity.

STRATEGY 27

Time Out for Kudos

101 Ways to Say "Very Good"

Q: We're ready for something completely different. When is it the right time to compliment someone?

A: Right now.

Here's a list developed by Dr. Roger Firestien and his colleagues at Buffalo State College's Center for Studies in Creativity. Dr. Firestein's books and tapes are available from: United Educational Services, PO Box 1099, Buffalo, NY14052 or call 1-800-458-7900.

1. You're right!
2. Good work!
3. Well done!
4. You did a lot of work today!
5. It's a pleasure to work with you.
6. Now you have it.
7. Fine job!
8. That's right!
9. Neat!
10. Super!
11. Nice going.
12. That's coming along nicely.
13. That's great!
14. You did it that time!
15. Fantastic!
16. Terrific!
17. Good for you!
18. You out-did yourself.
19. That's better.
20. Excellent.
21. That's good.
22. Good job.
23. That's your best work yet.

24. Good going.
25. That's really nice.
26. WOW!
27. Keep up the good work.
28. Outstanding!
29. Much better.
30. Good for you!
31. You're really talented.
32. Good thinking!
33. Exactly right!
34. You make it look easy.
35. I've never seen anyone do it better!
36. You're doing much better today.
37. Way to go.
38. Superb!
39. You're getting better every day.
40. You're right on target.
41. I knew you could do it.
42. Wonderful!
43. You're great!
44. Beautiful work!
45. You've worked hard.
46. That's the way!
47. Keep trying.
48. That's it.
49. Nothing can stop you now.
50. You're very good at that.
51. You're learning fast.
52. You certainly did well today.
53. I'm happy to see you working like that.
54. Keep it up!
55. I'm proud of you.
56. That's the way.
57. You're learning a lot.
58. That's better than ever.
59. Quite nice.
60. You've figured it all out.
61. Perfect!
62. Fine!

63. Your brain is in gear today.
64. You've got it!
65. You figured that out fast.
66. Very resourceful.
67. You really are improving.
68. Look at you go.
69. You've really got that down pat.
70. Tremendous!
71. I like that.
72. I couldn't do better myself.
73. Now that is what I call a fine job.
74. You did that very well.
75. Impressive!
76. Sharp!
77. Right on!
78. That's wonderful.
79. You mastered that in no time.
80. How nice.
81. Congratulations!
82. That was first-class work.
83. Sensational.
84. RIGHT!
85. You don't miss a thing.
86. You make my job fun.
87. You must have been practicing it.
88. I'm glad I assigned this to you.
89. You came through again.
90. DYNAMITE!
91. I knew I could count on you.
92. You deserve a raise.
93. How can I help you with this?
94. Go for it!
95. You bring sunshine into my life.
96. You have my complete support.
97. MARVELOUS!
98. Clever idea.
99. You are really on the ball.
100. I'm glad you're on our team.
101. I love your work.

SECTION IV

HOW TO GET HIRED

STRATEGY 28

Where Do You Start?

The days of one job per lifetime are over — you will have many different jobs, even career changes during the prime of your life. It's now estimated that the average American will have 7 - 10 different positions in his or her lifetime.

You are no longer tied to one career, thanks to transferable skills. There is a higher level of education today, we've gone from the horse and buggy to rockets to the moon in one century — imagine what the next will bring! We're in a fast-changing situation, and you need to be very adaptable.

You only have one chance here on Earth, so make sure you're doing something that you love.

STRATEGY 29

The Hidden Job Market

Let's talk about the hidden job market. New chapter, new verse, same old tune. The hidden job market is where the majority of new positions are discovered — the 85-95% of jobs *not* listed in the Sunday paper. We've hit upon a few of the markets already in the networking chapters, because these positions are filled by contacts, by being in the right place at the right time. Luck, you say? Yes, but we're showing you how to create your *own* luck!

The following statistics come from the Camil study of job search methods:

Job Search Method Through Which Job Was Obtained

Friends/Relatives	30.7%
Employer Direct	29.8
Answered Ad	16.6
Private Agency	5.6
Employment Service	5.6
Business Associates	3.3
School Placement	3.0
Labor Unions	1.4
Other	4.0
TOTAL	100.0

As Albert Einstein said, "In the middle of every difficulty lies an opportunity, a chance to find what you're after." Essentially, this entire book is structured to help you find that hidden job market, that hidden client market, and the (almost) perfect career!

STRATEGY 30
In the Beginning

In the beginning, you need to create the perfect document. The piece of paper that's going to get you through that door, give the employer a vision of greatness, and give you the chance to GET THAT JOB. Easier said than done?

The first step to designing the winning resume and cover letter is to write. List every accomplishment you've made in your career to date. Tell me everything, from how you made this company better to the achievements you made in the college drama club. From this list, we'll draw skills — transferable skills. Teaching a class or being a camp counselor can provide you with interpersonal relations skills, maybe certain projects you've undertaken have required research and evaluation skills.

There are hundreds of things you do every day that can be considered valuable by a potential employer — you just have to discover them. By writing them out, you can have an objective second party view these tasks and pick out ones that may have more merit than others. You're discovering reasons that an employer could hire you.

Notice that I use the word "could" instead of "should" — there's a good reason for that. I think of "should" as a weasel word — you're demanding something when you're not in a position to be bargaining. On the other hand, "could" provides the employer with a choice — you'll win him over with reasoning, not with your opinions.

From your list of achievements, come up with 10 reasons that an employer would hire you — people skills, writing ability, mathematical talent, honesty, dedication, flexibility. We're looking to develop a list of strengths that can be used in both the documents **and** during the interview (but that's another chapter!).

While you're doing this, come up with one weakness that you will then turn into a positive. If your weakness is procrastination, you can begin working on it *today;* if it's shyness, sign up for a class on public speaking; whatever the weakness is, turn it into something positive by taking action on it. This way, when a potential employer asks for your weaknesses, you don't lie and say you don't have any, nor do you ruin your chances for getting the job by telling him all of your sins. You are honest with him, and make a good impression for being willing to work on improving your mistakes.

STRATEGY 31

Discover Your USP

And Let the Word Out With Your Cover Letter!

Using your list of accomplishments, develop your own Unique Selling Position. What sets you apart from the competition — why would someone hire you to be a part of their team? This could be the theme of your cover letter: you are the perfect candidate for XYZ company, and here's why. Don't talk about what you've done in the past without relating it to future possibilities.

When putting together the cover letter, make it clean and fast. Tell the employer right away why it's worth his while to call you, and he'll read further. Don't be modest — sell yourself. You're the hottest product on the market today, and see to it the employer realizes that in the first few seconds of reading your material. Tell him how you can make money for him, save money for him, and get the job done! Tell him why he's reading this letter.

The average interviewer spends 30 seconds or less going over a cover letter and resume. Blind newspaper ads receive hundreds of replies that begin with the same line: **"I'm interested in the position of XYZ that you advertised in Sunday's paper."** No kidding. Don't tell that prospect something he already knows — tell him why you're applying, what you can do for him when you're hired. That will get his attention, and hopefully, get you in that door.

At the close of the cover letter, make a call for action. Give them a number to reach you, and tell them when it would be convenient. No one likes to waste time making phone calls, make it as easy as possible for the employer to contact you. Answering machines are worth every penny when you're looking for a better job.

After the signature, I'll add a P.S. — it's another attention-grabber, and it's a great way to personalize the letter. People read headlines and the P.S. — and if the middle copy is interesting enough, they'll cover that, too. But I like to use a P.S. just to be sure that they know I want their attention.

Take it personally—you should ALWAYS address your cover letters to an individual (except, of course, in the instance of a blind ad, which we'll cover later). Get the title, the address, the correct spelling of the names. What's the first thing you do when you receive mail that has your name spelled incorrectly? You probably laugh, and then don't take the piece (or its message) too seriously. Make sure that every part of the address is correct — every employer is looking for someone who pays attention to detail. They want to know that you're at least interested enough in their company to get the name and location right.

STRATEGY 32

Resumes: Your Ticket to the Ball

The same rules apply to resumes that apply to cover letters when it comes to keeping them short and simple. Make the objective powerful. In this age of the laser printer, it's easy enough to change a few words and have a couple of objectives. You want the person's attention immediately—tell them what you're looking for so they have the right idea up front.

I like to use bullets (•) to keep the copy flowing, make it easy on the eye, and keep the reader going to the end of the page. Use action words like "directed," "coordinated," " organized," and "managed" whenever appropriate.

A few words that will beef up any resume are the 12 selling

terms from *PowerSpeak* by Dorothy Leeds. The most powerful words in the English language are as follows:

Discovery	Safety
Easy	Money
Guarantee	New
Health	Save
Proven	Love
Results	You

These words will incite the reader to take action. On the other hand, words to avoid are: maybe, if, might, possibly, perhaps, and like. Stay away from wimpy words, and choose decisive, confident phrases.

The statements that you make are going to carry a lot of weight, so make them concise and to the point. Always use accomplishments—saying "Handled accounts receivable and payable" isn't as attention-grabbing as "Designed new structure for more efficient accounts receivable/payable system." The employer wants to know what you're capable of, and you can demonstrate this by listing your achievements.

You're putting your best foot forward, so don't be modest. I'm certainly not advocating stretching the truth, because your perfect job isn't one that you're not qualified for — you'll be miserable if you are not truthful with the prospective employer. If your abilities don't match the requirements, then your job performance will not make anyone happy, including YOU!

STRATEGY 33
Types of Tickets

Resumes can be chronological or functional — I prefer the chronological. That employer wants to know where you've worked, what you've done, and what you've accomplished. You should be able to list your skills in bulleted copy underneath the listing of company, city, years you've worked, and your title. Give the person the information they want right up front — don't make them hunt for it.

Many people feel that functional resumes are a good option, I've known people who've used that type, and what they've found is that the employer wants to know *where* they obtained these skills — did they actually use them on a job, did they take a class, or did they just read a book on the subject? She has no way of knowing, so I like to make it easy on her by telling her right away what I did, where I did it, and for how many years. She'll find my skills, and see how they've developed over the years when I use a chronological resume.

FOR YOUR REVIEW

I'm enclosing a copy of my resume for your comments on its style, content, and readability for the small fee of $39.95. I understand that I am not obligated to any further purchases. Please give me your thoughts and return the paperwork to:

Please type or print:

Your Name ____________________________________

Address ______________________________________

City ______________________State______Zip __________

Phone Number (   ) ____________________________

Payment Form:

❑ Check or Money Order Enclosed

❑ MC ❑ Visa # ________________________________

Expiration Date ________________________________

Cardholder's signature __________________________

Mail to: Kurt Barnaby Kojm, Senior Vice President
About-Face Executive Marketing
1833 Kensington Avenue
Buffalo, NY 14215

Fold Here

Place
Stamp
Here

Kurt Barnaby Kojm, Senior Vice President
About-Face Executive Marketing
1833 Kensington Avenue
Buffalo, NY 14215

STRATEGY 34

It *Is* the Size That Counts

The size of your resume, that is. Most people can (and do) use a one-page or 1 ½ page format. The 1 ½ page format is a little more professional — it helps you really stand out from the others. We list your name, address, and your employment objectives on the first flap, and inside we detail your experience, education, interests, and activities. It gives you a little more room than a one-page resume, and can be visually a bit less closed-in if you have a lot of experience.

The one-page is perfect for students who are just graduating, or for someone who's been at the same company for a number of years. You don't want a "cramped" resume, but one with too much "white space" is not the answer, either. The one-page format is pretty straightforward, just make sure that it's easy to read and flows well.

If you have an extensive amount of experience, a two-page resume is a good idea. In our case, it's printed as one 11x17 piece, and folded to make two 8 ½x11 halves (newsletter-style). I avoid stapling the two pages because this breaks up the copy, and the reader is not always going to turn that page. In the case of our document, the reader's eye automatically goes from the bottom of the inside left page to the top of the right. Again, be sure that you have enough information to make using this style worthwhile.

Sample Resumes

One Page

1 ½ Page

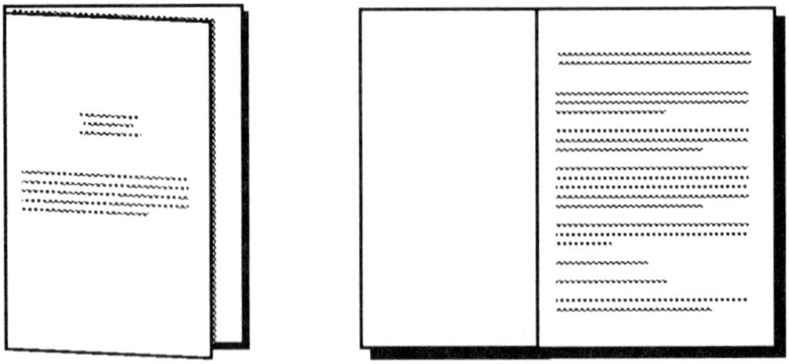

Front

Inside

2 ½ Page

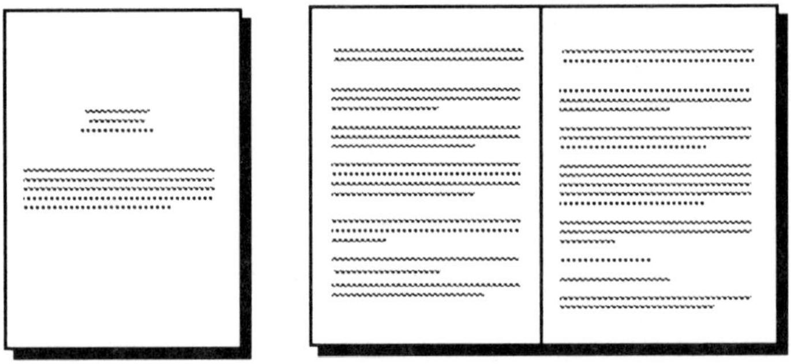

Front

Inside

STRATEGY 35

What's Your Favorite Color?

In the direct-mail business, we've found that off-white parchment has the highest readability. You can use grey, beige, or ivory, but I feel that white is too "stark" and cold. It's also a common color, so using a nice parchment in a slightly different shade will pull the reader's attention to your document.

Always use black ink on your resumes — black also tested highest for readability. Stay away from reds, blues, or browns, your readership may fall off significantly. Your cover letter can also use black ink, and be done on the same paper stock as your resume, if possible.

The resume can be laser-printed to avoid spotty or messy-looking copies. This will prove to the employer that you're detail-oriented when they look at someone's copy of a copy of a typewritten paper, and compare it to your crisp, clean document.

STRATEGY 36

The Mystery Document

This document will open many doors to you, and will set you far apart from the other candidates. Only one in a thousand individuals will actually take the trouble to put one of these together — and probably only one in a thousand individuals really has the perfect job. I think there's a direct correlation.

What do lawyers use, police search for, and applicants forget to bring to the interview? EVIDENCE.

Letters of testimonial from former employers, instructors, and clients should be collected, beginning with your first job or internship. These recommendations can be put into a book for review by potential clients or employers as references to the type and quality of work that you've produced.

Try to secure these letters at the time you've completed an outstanding project, had a good evaluation, or are leaving a company on good terms. If the supervisor doesn't have the time or inclination to write one, offer to compose one for him. He can then just put it on company stationery, and sign it.

These books are a tremendous asset when going on interviews or appointments with prospective clients. Keep copies of all of the letters so that if the employer wants to file them with your resume, he can.

Other material you may want in these books includes projects you've worked on, publications you've written, events you've participated in, seminars you've led, etc. It's actually a sort of professional scrap book on yourself and your years in the workforce. EVIDENCE SELLS!

STRATEGY 37

Personnel Agencies - the Cons and Pros

The Cons

Personnel (employment) agencies get paid for matching candidates to job openings. Occasionally, you'll find an agency looking for *clients* in a certain field, and what they'll do is creatively run an ad for a job that doesn't exist — or in a field that they don't have candidates for just yet. The reasoning is that if the employers see the agency's name out there, they'll think the agency is hot in the field, and contact them. Meanwhile, you've sent your resume, and you're hoping for a position that doesn't even exist.

Perhaps it's a job that a company created a few months ago, then dropped the idea. The agency will try to resurrect the position by bringing the manager a handful of resumes from qualified people, and saying "let's try again."

The Pros

On the plus side, there are many reputable agencies that can help you in your job search. A phone call is the easiest way to determine whether they place personnel in your field of interest. Tell them what your qualifications are, and be honest about the type of job you're after. The greatest advantage of using a firm like this is that you can learn a lot more about the corporation and the position before you spend time on an interview. The pre-screening policy is designed to save the employer time and money, but it certainly benefits you to discover the basics of an opening before the interview.

Employment agencies are excellent centers for practicing interviewing and follow-up skills. **Remember that only 5% of all jobs come through placement agencies**, but when you network with the pros, you'll add value to everything you handle.These people are around town every day, and they do want to place you in a job that you'll be happy with. Use interviews with these agencies to ask for feedback on the type of impression you're leaving.

STRATEGY 38

Newspaper Ads — Classified Information

Let's say it's a blind ad in the Sunday paper — that very night, and maybe Monday morning, everyone who's interested in that ad will be answering it. By Tuesday or Wednesday, there's a wave of paper engulfing Mr. Employer. After opening three or four of these, he'll have resume-itis. He'll narrow down the criteria, and start eliminating on this basis. Your paperwork may be too hard to read, you may have listed your high school and he's looking for a bachelor's degree, or maybe it's a poor copy and the staple is coming off. For whatever reason, your ticket to the ball is going to be disgarded.

One way to avoid this trap is to send your materials in the following week. This strategy helps you to avoid the paper wave, and will ensure that the employer will pay more attention to your resume than to the initial 100 he received the week before. Another attention-getter is to use a large envelope — very few people will use this method, and your resume and cover letter will stay crisp and clean. You'll stand tall above the rest before the envelope is even opened!

The resume is a double-edged sword — it can save you, fighting your way into the office for that interview, or it can kill you, piercing your heart by being thrown away without consideration of your qualifications.

Standing out from the crowd may also be achieved by not even sending your resume right away. Make yourself different by sending a wedding invitation or monarch-sized envelope. It will look unusual in the stack of mail, and compel the employer to open it. You might say something on the card like "Dear Employer, I'm currently updating my paperwork, here are four reasons that you could hire me...Let's get together soon. Sincerely," and sign it. Put a PS with your phone number on it, and get your resume ready for an interview!

Here's an example of the quick note we talked about:

```
Dear Employer:

I'm updating my paperwork. These are
four reasons why you could hire me:

1. I will make you money.
2. I will save you money.
3. You'll like my work.
4. I get the job done on time and
   in-budget.
I can be reached at 1-800-555-5555.

                 Sincerely,

                 Kurt Kojm

P.S. - When can we meet?
```

STRATEGY 39

Use the Newspaper For More Than Lining Bird Cages

Let's explore the possibilities of the local business paper. A weekly journal can provide you with lots of clues in the search for a perfect job. Get a fast glance at what's happening in your community, and look at the ads that local companies are producing. You may be able to create an opportunity for yourself by finding out what the company is selling, and discovering a method of improving upon that. If the company is selling dishes, find a better way to sell them, come up with a proposal or an idea, and send it off. Grab their attention. Start thinking about how you can help market that company better, help it grow, discover their unique selling position or, better still, create one for them. Tell them how you will make a difference to their company.

I like newspapers because they're very current. They keep you up-to-date on all of a company's actions, unlike the directories at the library.

You may want to call on the editors or reporters for more information — or to offer your own. Position yourself as an expert in the field, become your own public relations vehicle.

Here are some of the sections that you may find helpful in your search for the hidden job market:

Movers and Shakers

Use the "People on the Move" and "Awards and Achievements" sections to feel out potential contacts. These individuals are the movers and shakers of the town — write them a note of congratulations, and ask how they can help you on your own job search. Look at the companies that are growing, that are promoting people. Usually a company must hire someone to fill the position of a person being promoted. If your skills seem similar, drop that individual or company a line.

New Hire Newswire

Pay particular attention to the former place of employment of the newly-hired individual. This means that the company is probably looking for a replacement. The normal period of notice for leaving a company is 2 weeks, and that's not nearly enough time for an employer to advertise, interview, hire, and train a person. You may get in there just a bit ahead of the competition, and save the employer time and money right away!

The Workshop is Coming, The Workshop is Coming

Other avenues for using the newspaper are announcements of conventions or seminars coming to town. As I've mentioned before, these gatherings are a great source of leads as well as educational information in a field that interests you.

It Ain't Necessarily So

Check the bankruptcies for your own protection, but also for potential goldmines, especially if you're into financial planning. One person's disaster can be another person's gold. Also look at the judgments and liens. These are people who need help, and by being a hero, you can increase your network while adding to your credibility. It's another example of the hidden job market that's right in front of us every day.

There's No Business Like New Business

The "New Business" section is very valuable. New businesses need services, from interior design to water coolers to accounting. Find out what their needs are, and meet them.

What's Your Opinion?

The editorial pages (as well as "Lifestyle" and "Sports") provide you with an alternative point of view, broaden your background, and stimulate your thinking. They're good places to cover.

"Ad" It Up

Advertisements throughout the paper tell you who's spending the marketing dollars in the community, especially those running color ads. They're investing a lot, and you can be sure that they're actively seeking participation in the marketplace. Come up with ideas for them, and send them off. See what happens.

STRATEGY 40
Other Publications

Other publications you may consider reference tools are the Yellow Pages (great for finding competitors and leaders in a variety of fields); Ad Facs (in Upstate New York, a great directory of marketing services); the Thomas Directory of Manufacturing; and any newsletters put out by local organizations or corporations that you may be interested in joining or pursuing.

Most important, corporate brochures and annual reports are a great source of information, especially when it comes to Fortune 500 companies. **Stay out of the personnel department**. Mailing your resume to "personnel" instead of an individual significantly lowers your chances of getting in the door. The Fortune 500 companies receive somewhere between 250,000 to 1,000,000 pieces of mail from people who want positions there. To better your chances of being noticed, find out who the vice president of your chosen department is, and send it to him or her. If it's marketing, look for the marketing director or communications manager; if you're interested in accounting, there's a head of that section who will possibly read your resume and cover letter more closely than the person in human resources who gets thousands every day. Actually, the only time you *could* send your material to personnel is if that's the department you want to work for!

Icebreakers
21 Questions for the Prospective Employer

Here are 21 potential questions to raise in your interview:

1. How do you see yourself in the marketplace?
2. Who is perceived as the leader?
3. In which direction do you see the company growing over the next 2 - 3 years?
4. How are you adding value to your present product line?
5. Which direction is the department heading?
6. Where do you see the company's greatest challenge?
7. How would you improve it?
8. If you could do anything, what would you do to make it better?
9. Which resources do you have?
10. What kind would you use if they were available?
11. What's on your wish list?
12. Why would you start a program like XX?
13. Who would you want on your team?
14. Where would you find them?
15. What's your destination?
16. How soon would you do it?
17. Is this a new position?
18. What happened to my predecessor?
19. Is there anything else you want to know about me?
20. Based on the qualifications you've heard so far, do I have the qualifications you're looking for?
21. You **will** recommmend me, won't you?

Practice, practice, practice again, in front of friends, family, and mirrors, too.

SECTION V

• • • • • • • • • • •

INTERVIEWING

STRATEGY 41
Dress To Impress

Ask ten different people what you should wear to an interview, and you'll get ten different answers. There are books upon books available on this subject, but what I've found is that usually, common sense is the best measure of good taste.

In general, blue or grey suits are appropriate. A solid or small print shirt or blouse works best — you want the interviewer to focus on YOU and your qualifications, not your outfit! It goes without saying that your clothes need to be freshly laundered, your shoes shined, and your personal hygeine attended to. I would not recommend wearing perfume or cologne, unless it's used in moderation. Avoid (at all costs) wearing suits that don't quite fit — whether they're too tight or too large. That interviewer is going to be looking at how you'll present yourself to *her* clients, and she'd better be impressed!

Remember, these tips on dressing for the initial interview also apply to your appearance once you've been hired. Additionally, Herb Knoll, in his book *The Total Executive,* recommends that executives keep grooming accessories (toothbrush, razors, toothpaste, etc.) at the office; that they keep a fresh shirt available; and to avoid wearing running shoes to an office or party.

STRATEGY 42

Most Frequently Asked Questions

In the interview, you should do all the talking, right? The spotlight's on you, right? Wrong. In this situation, you ought to try to keep the employer talking about themselves and their needs, and then try to match your skills and abilities to those needs. It's much more effective when you do the interviewing, so to speak. The ratio should actually be **80%** active listening to **20%** answering questions—just make sure that that 20% is used optimally, and fully expresses your strengths and potential benefit to the company.

What I recommend prior to an interview is going through a list of questions that you need to be prepared for, and practicing your responses. Here are the most frequently asked questions by future employers:

1. **Tell me a little about yourself.**
2. **What are your weaknesses?**
3. **Why do you want to work for my corporation?**
4. **Why did you leave your last job?**

My suggestion is to take the initiative and have the answers scripted out beforehand. Write out your responses, and practice them. Keep in mind that employer's favorite station is WII-FM (What's In It For Me?) — this is what he's tuned into 24 hours a day, 7 days a week. If you can tune in to this frequency, you'll be hired. Being prepared is going to make a big difference, so be sure that your answers are concise, sharp, and impressive to the listener.

STRATEGY 43
The Three Kissing Cousins

The Three Kissing Cousins - question one from Strategy 43 may be phrased in a number of ways: **"Tell me a little about yourself," "Why could I hire you?"** and **"Tell me your strengths."** The employer wants to know what separates you from the pack — why you stand out from the other candidates for this position. Your answer (scripted out and practiced well in advance) can include your education, experience, and skills positioned in the most succinct way possible. "Well, my B.A. in communications was completed in only three years, I have had five years of experience in the public relations field at *Fortune 500* firms, and my written and oral communications skills are outstanding." You've just wrapped yourself into a neat little package, and you've done a great job selling it. Keep the answers short and interesting, and leave it to the employer to expand on them.

STRATEGY 44
Negate the Weakness Trap

"What are your weaknesses?" — the dreaded question from the future employer. Do you say you don't have any, and let him think you have something to hide? Or do you unload your problems, and hope she'll be understanding? My recommendation is to give them a weakness, but turn it into a positive — "My communications skills are tops. If I had a weakness, it used to be procrastination. What I do now is practice time management skills — I write things down, prioritize them, and get them done. And my organizational skills have also improved as a result." What you've done is taken a weakness and spun it around to become another strength. You started with a strength, put a weakness in the middle, and ended with a positive.

Never dwell on negatives — it's an easy way to disqualify yourself from a position. **Highlight your skills that can make 'em money, save 'em money, build relationships, and complete projects.** If the interviewer has a lot of people applying for a job, he's actually looking for reasons not to hire you, so don't give him a hand by going on and on about your weaknesses.

STRATEGY 45
The Shmooz Question

Why do you want to work for ABC Corporation? Because you need the money, because you always wanted to be an architect, because you heard they have an opening? These are **not** strong responses! "No one cares how much you know until they know how much you care."

If you've done your homework on the corporation, bring up something that really impressed you in their material. "I noticed that sales in 1989 were up 20% from 1988, and I know that you'll be introducing a new product soon. It sounds like your sales force is outstanding, and that's the kind of team I want to be a part of!" That interviewer will be very impressed.

You could also mention something about the people you've noticed in the office — the way that they communicate easily and seem to work together well. Make sure you notice that company's USP (Unique Selling Position), and mention it when answering this question. Keep your eyes open at all times from the moment you walk in the front door. **Monitor the activities of the staff — do they look happy or overworked; are people working together or individually; do they seem friendly and interact well, or do they keep to themselves? Notice how others are treated in the organization, and make sure that this is what you want for yourself.**

CHAPTER 46
TO TELL THE TRUTH
(Or Not To Tell the Truth)

That is the question. "Why did you leave your last position?" Do they really want to know that your boss was a hyperactive maniac who treated you like a dog? Did they offer you a rubber biscuit instead of a bonus? That your office was so small you could stand in the middle and touch both walls? That your paycheck was so small that you needed a microscope to find it? No. This is not what they want to hear.

If you speak poorly of former employers, most interviewers will fear you'll talk that way about their company if things do not work out. Telling them that you were fired from your last three jobs may demonstrate your honesty, but it won't get you hired.

On the other hand, you have to have a good reason for leaving your present job. "I'm looking for a greater challenge" is a pat line that these people hear every day. Try something different like "I want to use my marketing skills more than I am now. I have a strong aptitude for budgeting that I don't feel is being used to its full potential, and I know that your marketing position mentioned accounting skills in the job description."

Be as honest as you can, without digging your own grave. The interviewer knows there are problems at your present job or you wouldn't be looking for a new one, so don't give him any ammunition against you.

Again, practice, practice, practice. Stop right now, put down this book and march to the nearest mirror. Ask yourself why you left your last position. Are you smiling?

STRATEGY 47

The Final Question

"Do you have any questions?" Most people will say "no" and leave it at that. You can choose to be different. This is your time to take center stage and shine!

Take a 3x5 index card before the interview, and list five questions you want to ask. Go through the corporation's brochure, and come up with interesting facts to ask about, preferably ones that relate to the job opening. Ask the interviewer "how long do we have?" Adapt your presentation accordingly.

Don't try to commit these questions to memory — if you draw a blank at the end of a pretty trying interview, you're out of luck.

Besides, the employer will be impressed with your preparation skills and genuine interest in his company and the position available. This technique emphasizes your organizational skills, time management talents, and value skills.

Also on these cards, you may include your strength statements in case they don't come up in the interview. They may be specific abilities that suit this corporation, and ones that you know are important to bring out in the initial interview. Rather than remembering them while driving home, write them out on these 3x5 cards, and have it right in front of you.

Some of the questions you may want to ask could be: "What do you consider this organization's greatest strength?" and "How did you get hired? What was it like?" These will get the person talking about their favorite subject (themselves) and help them to warm up to you.

A good technique to use after you've asked the questions on the 3x5 card, or at any time during the interview, is what Jeff Slutsky termed "echoing." It's actually a form of active listening where you subtly repeat what the interviewer is saying back to him. You can also use "OK" or "Oh?" to keep the conversation slanted toward the interviewer. Practice this with a friend — how long did the conversation continue?

STRATEGY 48
Your Finale

Get the interviewer into the habit of saying "yes." "Does this make sense?" "Do you see where my skills can benefit this organization?", "Of everything you've heard so far, do you see a match between my skills and your corporation?", "Based on the evidence you've heard so far, do you see where my talents can help you?" and finally, the killer — **"You will recommend me, won't you?"**

If the answer is "yes," find out what the next step is. Who will you interview with next, when are they available? If it's not today, ask the interviewer how you can strengthen your presentation. What are his recommendations for impressing the next person? Get feedback, and use it to your advantage.

If the answer is "no," ask him who he knows that could help you on your job search. Discover what he thought the weaknesses of your presentation were, and how he would improve it for the next one. People like to feel important, and by showing him that you value his opinions, he will more than likely try to help you. And if nothing else, you've added another link to your network chain.

STRATEGY 49

The Million Dollar Question

Salary is usually a major concern both of the employer and the interviewee. Don't bring up the subject first, and if at all possible, let them give you a price range before you tell them what you're looking for. If you mention $30,000 and the actual pay range is $35 - 40,000, you've just cut yourself down. There's also the danger in perceived value — if the employer sees you looking for less money, he may think that you don't have the necessary skills or experience.

On the other hand, if the salary is $30,000 and you say $35,000 (being optimistic), you'll be disqualified. They may feel that you're overqualified, and that you wouldn't be happy making less than you expected — even if it's a job you'd love. It's hard to convince people that you'd be happier making less than you are now, even if it's the truth!

Once an offer is made, try to get it in writing. They may be dancing around a figure, but not have the authority to make that decision. If you see an offer in writing, it's a solid bid from the firm.

One strong negotiation technique is to thank them for the offer, and ask for two weeks to consider it. You put a little fear into them — they may up the ante, you may get another offer. Job offers are like rabbits — you get one, you'll get another, then another, and another, and another. The law of attraction usually surfaces, so don't jump at the first offer.

27 Ways to Ask for the Job

The following have been adapted from a list found in Joe and Judy Sabah's book *How to Get The Job You Really Want And Get Employers to Call You*. Here are 27 ways to "close the sale" by asking for the job. For more information, contact Joe or Judy Sabah, PO Box 101330, Denver, Colorado 80250. Call (303) 722-7200.

1. When would you like me to start?
2. Where will I work? (Desk, etc.)
3. Who will be my boss?
4. When would you like me to meet some of my co-workers?
5. Thank you for the interview, I would really like to have this job.
6. It would be really nice to have this job.
7. Do you think I have a chance for this job?
8. The office, benefits, etc. are super, and I think I would like to make my career here.
9. Do I have the job?
10. I can start as soon as possible.
11. Where would I be sitting?
12. I can start today if you want.
13. I will do my very best for your company.
14. I would be very happy working here.
15. The office seems like a pleasant place to work.
16. Both you and I can gain.
17. What time should I be here?
18. Thank you, I hope I will be working with you.
19. What time tomorrow would you like me to come in?
20. Will I be working Monday through Friday?
21. How many employees do you have now?
22. I think I would be an asset to your company.
23. I can't wait to start working here.
24. When can I call back to find out when I can start?
25. During the first week, can I look around and familiarize myself with the office and how it runs?
26. Will I be working full- or part-time?
27. Do you feel I am qualified for this job?

Brain Games

These games are designed to show you just how easy change can be — and how much of a difference it can make!

1. 3 I II6	Add four strokes to create a loud noise.
2. 3 II 6	Add two strokes to make an insect.
3. OOII	Add three strokes to make a gold miner's dish.
4. II 030	Add two strokes to create a displaced person.
5. II O II O	Add three strokes to create man
6. 3 IOI O II I	Add eight strokes to make a two-winged airplane.
7. 9I II I	Add five strokes to make an adhesive substance.
8. II I I	Add two strokes and make nothing.

More games:

Q: A man gave a cashier a card with the number 102004180 and walked out the door. Why didn't he pay?

A: Because it read "I ought to owe nothing for I ate nothing."

9. ooo	Add two strokes and make a soda.
10. ooo	Add three strokes to create a father.
11. 9 I II	Add three strokes to make a weapon.
12. I IOI I	Add four strokes to create a mother.

Connect the dots with four lines that all touch and your pen cannot leave the paper.

See page 77 for answer

1. BANG 2. BUG 3. PaN 4. HOBO
5. HOMO 6. BIpLaNE 7. gLUE
8. NIX 9. pop 10. dad 11. gUN
12. MOM

SECTION VI

THE FOLLOW-UP

STRATEGY 50

Follow Me, Follow My Advice...and Follow Up

Every day, thousands of people read the want ads, network with clients, send in resumes, and go on interviews. Only a few hundred of these people will probably be hired. Why? Because they stand out from the rest, **they prove to the employer that they're worth hiring *before* they're actually hired.**

One terrific way to do this is to follow up with that prospect. Show her that you're persistent, you're hard working, and that you'll get the job done. The next few chapters outline methods for following up a spectacular interview. **Good luck!**

STRATEGY 51
Dialing For Dollars

To follow up the original paperwork, you should always call in. Whether your resume has been requested or is just being sent blind, a quick call to ensure that it was received will set you apart from the rest.

Remember that telephone skills are very important. You must sound confident, believable, and competent when talking to these people. Using "um" and "you know" immediately decreases your effectiveness, and makes you seem less credible and interesting.

Direct mail marketers have found that you can double your response rate by simply making a call. They will tell you that they're lucky to have a 1 or 2% return on 100 pieces sent out — but by following up with a phone call, they can increase the odds by 5, 6, or 7%.

Other "phone tricks" — fax a picture of a telephone (with you on it) along with a short note. Or mail a box with a mini-telephone and enclose a note that highlights what's in it for them if they hire you.

Understand that I am not advocating making a pest of yourself — remember, you want to be on the interviewer's or client's good side. And if you're responding to an ad that says "no calls," pay attention. They may automatically disqualify you if you cannot follow directions before you're even hired!

Answer to puzzle from previous page

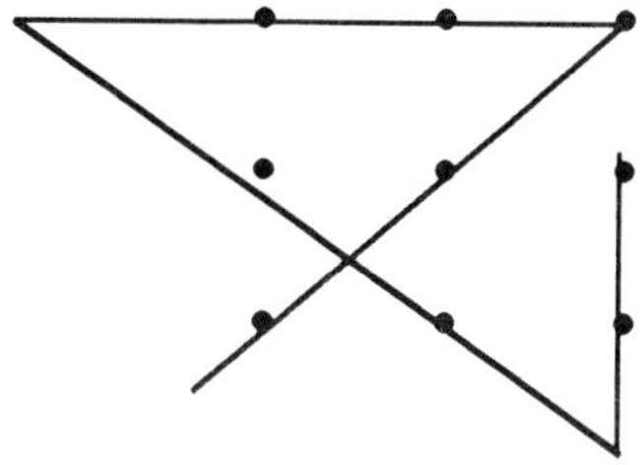

STRATEGY 52

Passing the Screen Test

OK, you've sent your materials and want to follow up, but you can't seem to get past the secretary. This is actually the sign of a good secretary, and most employers want the staff to do exactly what they're doing — screen people.

Your first step is to be friendly. Explain your situation to the secretary, find out when a good time to talk with Mr. Employer would be, and call at that time. Let the person know that her help is invaluable to you, and that you only need a few minutes of her boss's time for your telephone conversation.

You may want to try calling early in the morning or after usual working hours, or even during lunch. Most executives take advantage of this time for extra work. There's no secretary, so you'll get through more easily, and you could even make a pitch that tells him that he wouldn't have to work these hours if he hires you — you'll help him to make the department more efficient and effective, so overtime won't be necessary.

You can place a person-to-person call to the individual you're trying to reach. The operator can often bypass the secretary, and you only pay for the call if you speak to the person you wanted.

Another tactic is to say "Mr. Jones may be expecting my call." Try it, if she picks up on it, explain that you've sent your paperwork, and would like to discuss the possibility of doing a project with ABC Corporation further. If the secretary is on your side, she may be able to convince her superior that you are worth talking to. If she's not on your side, you'll have a very hard time getting through to him.

STRATEGY 53

The Importance of a Thank-You Card

ALWAYS send a thank-you card to people you've met with. I would estimate that 95% of the individuals I meet will say that they send these out, but only 5% actually do. The 5 minutes it takes to write a line and drop it in the mail will really help you stand out from the crowd.

Include a strong point that you may have come up with after the interview. If you talked about football, mention a play from their last game. You're building rapport, and trying to establish a friendship here.

Don't forget to ask for the order again. Close with "Thanks again. When can we meet to discuss this further?"

Teamwork pays big dividends. You can also include the secretary or assistant who may have been instrumental in getting you through that door — sending them a quick note of thanks can bring them onto your team forever!

STRATEGY 54

The Heavy Artillery - Lumpy Mail

Rick Barrera shaped this million-dollar idea which I use as a follow-up to a thank-you card. (Rick is a professional speaker from La Jolla, California. He is the co-author of the book *Non-Manipulative Selling.* I highly recommend it! It's full of ideas that a creative job hunter could use.) His lumpy mail idea will put you above even that 5% who *do* send a note after the interview. Don't use it immediately because it's very powerful — wait about a week or so.

The envelope can be any size, from a regular #10 to a tube mailer designed to look like a stick of dynamite. The address should be handwritten, and there should be an unusual stamp on it. You may even write a quote on it, something like "Inch by inch, anything is a cinch...Robert Schuller." From the outside, it will look interesting because it's personalized, and it's *lumpy!*

The lump itself can be anything, from candy to a pen to a cassette tape. The idea is to draw interest and encourage the prospect to open that envelope! NYNEX sent me a yellow page stationery holder for my desk (an expensive example); Tom Scioli's One Step Forms sent me a pen. You might send a lottery ticket— "Odds are, I'm a winner," "Both this ticket and I are one in a million," or "Hiring me is hiring a winner!" Be creative with the object, and keep in mind that the content of your letter is what's crucial.

In your note, enclose something related to a topic of mutual interest — something that concerns the company, what they produce or who they serve. Reverse roles — ask the employer "If you were me, how would you position yourself to help the firm?"

You should include "cc"s on the letter — carbon copy everyone within that hierarchal structure. It will get others involved in your cause, and talking about you and your work.

The following are suggestions for getting the most out of the lumpy mail strategy:

Hear Ye, Hear Ye

Clip an article or announcement of an upcoming seminar from a newspaper, business journal or magazine, and highlight it. Send it on to them with a note — "What do you think about this? I found it in the Nightingale Conant catalog. Can we get together and talk about it?"

New Twist On an Old Product

You may come up with a new way to market an existing product—the invention of Silly Putty® came about through an entrepreneur who approached a chemical company about their waste goo that was formerly thrown away. The rest is history. You can look for other avenues of selling products under other titles to other markets.

Suppliers and Demanders

Locating better suppliers or new vendors for the prospect is a way of making two people very happy — and you make network links from both of them. You're acting as the eyes and ears of the prospective client/boss, and you've also become a "salesperson" for the vendor.

See It and Believe It

Videotape sells. If you see something that would interest your prospective client or employer, you can send a video as your lumpy mail technique. If this is too expensive, photographs work well also. You may even want to make your own videotape to send out — keep it simple, just you in front of the camera. Extravagance can backfire on you, so make it clean and crisp.

Listen Up

Audiotapes are great. In addition to creating a "lump," they are fairly easy to record on, and can get you noticed! It's a personal thing, and the executive can listen to it in the car, the office, or at home...at his convenience.

Take the Stub-Way

Tickets to a ballgame, the theater, or a concert can be used as a follow-up. We mentioned using them to grab a prospect's attention prior to an interview, but they actually work even better afterward. At the game, you can discuss projects in a relaxed, casual atmosphere, and have fun while building rapport.

Make an Issue

If you've noticed which publications your prospect reads, pick up a current issue. Use an article from this to include in your lumpy mail, or send him a subscription to a magazine you feel he'd be interested in reading. Again, build that rapport.

Here are a few ways to jazz up your actual mailing piece:

Sending the lumps registered mail or Federal Express is a bit costly, but will get the attention of the potential employer. You may also fax him a quick note after sending the lumpy mail.

A bounce-back mailer is a novel idea. Send a stamped, self-addressed reply card to your future employer, and make it easy for him to respond to you. Major corporations use these postage-guaranteed response cards, you can adopt their technique.

Use multiple stamps for mailing your materials. There are a number of unique postage possibilities, and the more stamps you have on a piece, the less likely the prospect is to throw it away. A well-known minister built his empire employing marketing tactics like this — it can surely work for you as well!

CHAPTER 55

Flowers From Heaven

Another technique to thank someone is to send flowers, especially if they did you a favor or went out of their way to see you. Don't get carried away and look like you're trying to bribe the person, but everyone loves flowers. If there is any way that your gesture will be misconstrued or misinterpreted, don't send them, pick another strategy.

Telegrams are also effective. They reach the right person, and get the message across in a short, to-the-point way.

Ann Marie Roll even sent potential employers pizza, sheet cakes, and chicken wings with her resume attached! You might sent your boss coffee with a note that says "coffee, cream, *and* me!" By cutting through the clutter, you position yourself as a "doer" who's on top of things.

STRATEGY 56
Turn Rejection Into Gold

What happens after you've hunted down the right job, interviewed with the top people, followed-up to the max, and then you get the dreaded REJECTION LETTER? Most people would throw it out or file it...but throughout this book, I've never told you to do what *most* people do, have I?

This rejection letter is a golden opportunity to get back in, make yourself a contact, and open new doors in uncharted waters. You have no way of knowing if the other candidate actually reported to work, if they are able to do what they said they could, or if there will soon be a new opening in a different department. There may even be a position with a firm that happens to be owned by the interviewer's best friend. Stranger things have happened!

My suggestion is to send the employer a note thanking them for considering you, and then ask them for help. "Who do you know that can help me in my job search? I'll call you on January 17th, but if you come up with anything in the meantime, please call me at 555-5555."

You're demonstrating perseverance, follow-up skills, and tenacity. You may even get a letter from them recommending you for a different position within the company. All it takes is the "ask." Know that people hire people, paper doesn't...your contact is out in the field every day, and could be aware of many opportunities in your areas of interest right in your own community. Making these people your friends will certainly help your job search move along more quickly.

SECTION VII

• • • • • • • • • • • • • • • • • • •

Standing Out

STRATEGY 57

Standing Out From the Crowd

If you always do what you've always done, you'll always get what you've always gotten! What makes you different than anyone else?

I'm trying to show you how to bend the rules a little — the rules that say to be conservative in your job-hunting approach. Use "what if" scenarios to determine whether some of these new approaches to the traditional employment search could work for you!

STRATEGY 58

The Personal Visit

One way to either approach or re-visit a prospect is to just "pop in." The personal visit is very time consuming, and it's a long-shot, but once in a while, it works.

These stops can also provide background information on the company, and help you to establish a better rapport with the secretary.

Friday afternoon is a great time to drop by, a lot of people put off starting projects because of the impending weekend. I've also found that Wednesday afternoons are also particularly productive. But at all costs, stay away from Monday mornings!

Try this technique and see if you are comfortable with it. If you're in sales, it should be a breeze, and you'll find yourself developing some good, solid skills. On the other hand, if you're not at ease just dropping in on prospects, you can revert back to our other tactics.

STRATEGY 59

Call 1-800-HIRE-YOU

To be very unique, you could install your own personal 800 number. "Phoning home" is a lot less costly for corporations, especially if you're trying to relocate to a new city. The actual price of installing and maintaining these numbers is not very high, compared to the results it can generate for you!

STRATEGY 60

Demonstrate Your Capabilities

Stage a demonstration outside of your targeted company, complete with picket signs that have "pro-corporation" slogans. Try to get the news media involved, and send it on to the CEO and Board of Directors. There's nothing like a little positive publicity to perk up a leader's interest.

STRATEGY 61

Sign It

Rent a vacant store window in the neighborhood of your prospective employer's corporation. Post signs in these windows that highlight your benefits to the company. "Hire me. I'm the best copywriter money can buy. 1-800-U-CALL-ME." Then send photographs of your project to the organization.

SECTION VIII

SPECIAL INTEREST GROUPS

STRATEGY 62

The Entrepreneur

Explore the opportunities of starting up your own company. Consult the Small Business Administration, the Chamber of Commerce, or other services designed to work with people who share your entrepreneurial spirit.

Whether it's a new invention, a restaurant venture, or a unique twist on a traditional company, there are endless possibilities for adventuresome individuals.

The key to success is to read at least 20 minutes a day. When you invest this time in yourself, you can finish 10 - 12 business books and magazines a year! That knowledge is power.

I'd also recommend using the Ben Franklin "T-Graph" that we discussed in earlier chapters. You should carefully study the pluses and minuses of risking your future. If you decide to go ahead, get all of the advice you can, from every person you can. Develop a strong strategic business plan that includes budgets, marketing strategies, and implementation procedures. Read all the publications you can about starting your own company, and let the information guide you down the path to greater wealth and happiness!

STRATEGY 63

The Over Fifty Force

If you're a part of this category, you're a mature worker with many years of experience. Your strengths may include a greater commitment to quality and more stability than a lot of younger people today.

Your network of contacts and resources should be a healthy one (if not, it's easy to build one). Companies will place more value on you as an employee if you position yourself correctly. You can bring your past experience along with your fresh ideas to today's workplace.

The employer may view the older employee as a rich source of skilled labor — costing the corporation less in training and making fewer mistakes than entry-level staff. There is usually less absenteeism with this group, as dedication to the company is still high on their list of values.

Providing role models to their younger counterparts, the over-50 force guides the energy of the youth, and makes things happen for the corporation.

STRATEGY 64

Teenagers

Around the age of 16 is when most people get their first experience with the world of work. My advice to today's young people is to *get involved.* Whether it's cutting lawns, delivering papers, or baby sitting, you're developing skills that will be valuable to an employer later in life. What's important is to just get out there and try something. This is the time in your life to discover what you like to do, as well as what you don't like.

There are a number of resources open to youth. Community groups like the Boy and Girl Scouts of America provide programs that teach children skills while they're having fun. These groups also encourage students to explore their own abilities and provide support for the interests that these kids express.

My own personal experience as an Eagle Scout has opened many doors for me as an adult — something I never would have considered when I was learning to tie knots, sail boats, and build bridges. These programs teach children the value of community service — there are so many good things that come out of giving service to others.

STRATEGY 65
Students

Students who are still in school should take every advantage of internship programs, work-study opportunities, and volunteer projects. These are all superb ways to gain the experience that companies are looking for while you're completing your education.

You can get involved in student government, local university chapters of student associations, and fraternities.

Call the United Way, get involved in local charities, take a leadership position on a project if possible. You'll be making a difference in the community, feeling good about yourself, making important contacts, learning skills, and gaining experience — all at the same time!

STRATEGY 66
College Graduates

There is nothing in one's career that can match the importance of graduation. One moment you're a student, and the next you've been transformed into a full-fledged member of society. There are so many opportunities open to you — where do you begin?

Well, this book should give you some pointers to get started. And let me give you this small insight: whoever hires you for the first couple of years after college will be *overpaying* you. That's right. Because essentially, they are providing your training — school really teaches you how to learn, and the employer is the one who hones your job skills and discovers your true abilities. However, when these skills have been acquired after a couple of years, you'll probably be underpaid for about the next 20!

So go ahead — launch your career. The obstacles that litter your path are actually learning opportunities, so you must take the initiative and get out there *now.*

STRATEGY 67

Re-Entering the Workforce

After years of being a chef, housekeeper, nurse, counselor, and cab driver, your children are all away at school and you're wondering what to do with your time. You're thinking of going back to work, so what's the first step?

Decide what it is that you truly love to do. Dig a little deeper, and pull out the skills that you've acquired that help you to do this work.

The next step is to decide which market your skills are suited to, and to go after it. You may want to take an adult-education class to update your abilities or even to further develop your talent.

Prepare your resume as I've outlined here, utilize a few of my winning strategies to get in the door, prepare for the interviews, and you'll be back to work in no time! (Just remember the old adage: "be careful what you wish for, you just might get it!" Make sure you're going after something that you really enjoy!)

You may even want to take a self-esteem course — everyone has a right to feel good about themselves. If you need a "jump

STRATEGY 68
The Armed Forces

I was asking the Armed Forces of the United States what they look for in candidates, and also what the candidates are looking for from the Armed Forces. The answers were not surprising, actually the two groups were mainly looking for the same thing — the recruits wanted: educational opportunities; leadership and management skills; the pride of being a member of an organization like the Armed Forces; to develop self-reliance, self-discipline, and self-direction; to seek out professional and developmental opportunities; and to achieve financial security and benefits. They are looking for the challenges that come with opportunities for travel and adventure. And the Armed Forces are looking for individuals who want that exact challenge.

STRATEGY 69
Salespeople

Salespeople are a unique breed. You're willing to go out there, take on extraordinary odds, and do anything to achieve your goals. You have tremendous research, design, planning, and interpersonal relations skills. The key to a great salesperson is their follow-through.

The majority of people will call on a prospect two or three times, but the average sale doesn't happen until the fifth, sixth, or seventh call. In the meantime, discouragement sets in, and everything becomes a battle of nerves. What you really need is faith in yourself, and to develop a persistent pattern that will bring you to that prospect's door over and over again, but always in unique and different ways. There are probably ten salespeople trying to get in to see her — you must stand out. Using some of the techniques in this book is a good way to start.

Using some of the techniques in this book is a good way to start. Eventually, you'll develop your own style, and once you "nail down" that first client, word of mouth will help to open more doors for you. Referrals are very powerful sales pieces, and can motivate clients to action like nothing else can.

Salespeople also have a number of alternatives to the "normal career." You can go into management, administration, or production. You are the "engine" of society — nothing happens until something is sold. Whether it's an idea, a tangible thing, or an event, it cannot exist without consumer demand.

One of the keys to being a great salesperson is to enjoy what you're doing. You must like, trust, and believe in the product or service that you're selling. Developing expertise in a field gives you credibility and will improve your sales, so you must choose a market that you're comfortable with.

Develop a unique selling position — why should Mr. and Mrs. Smith buy from you rather than the guy down the street? **What's in it for them?** Outline the benefits of working with you and your company clearly in the initial sales pitch. Do you provide better service, a more comprehensive warranty, a more competitive price? Say so right up front. Don't attack your competition, just explain your benefits and **SELL YOURSELF.**

STRATEGY 70
Teachers

In a way, teachers are another variety of sales people. You are selling knowledge, learning abilities, ideas, and thought patterns. The problem that I've noticed with many teachers who want to change jobs is that they suffer from low self-esteem. You may believe that teaching is all that you can do, and this is ridiculous.

The talent that it requires to become a teacher is incredible. In most cases, your counseling skills are top-notch — you have dealt with difficult students on all levels. You probably have lesson to the year-long schedule. Teachers also possess managerial skills like decision-making, motivating a team, and being a good role model.

My recommendation to teachers looking for a new job is to go back and discover your transferable skills. These can open up new frontiers for you. There is a danger with instructing positions in that people get into ruts. They get used to the security of their tenure, and are reluctant to take risks. You must explore some new alternatives if you're unhappy with what you're doing—you only go around once, and if you take away nothing else from reading this book, you have learned that doing what you love is the most important priority in your lifetime.

STRATEGY 71

Nurses

Nurses are angels from heaven, taking care of difficult people while working under strict guidelines and tremendous pressure. Nurses are a strong lot with a wealth of skills.

When it comes to employment, you can pick and choose virtually anything, from selling hospital equipment to administration to teaching. Your transferable skills are outstanding, ranging from interpersonal relations to organizational and time management. Nurses are skilled at counseling and guiding, so your listening abilities are top-notch.

The trap that I've seen people in this profession fall into is always yielding to a higher power, feeling inferior. These people need to take charge of their own lives, and use their outstanding personalities and individual strengths to their own advantage!

STRATEGY 72
Radio/TV Personalities

Virtually everyone's dream is to be on TV, but not everyone is prepared to do the work behind the scenes that's necessary to become successful.

A major part of the job of broadcast personalities is projecting the feeling of confidence. You are representing us, entertaining us, and mirroring us all at the same time. There is a great responsibility to yourself and your listeners, viewers, and readers to deliver the best.

From these talents, we can find transferable skills that could lend themselves to careers in public relations, management, and account handling. The ability to communicate clearly and effectively is a gift—and it's also a very marketable commodity in today's society.

I see broadcasters entering a variety of alternative positions: spokesperson, public service directors, public speaking, and fund-raising/development are only a few. There's also the customer service or hospitality angle. You may even find a career in writing in the advertising or public relations fields.

People in broadcasting also possess an inner excitement and enthusiasm for what you're doing. Employers are quick to pick up on that energy, and will want it to be harnessed for their company!

PERSONAL GROWTH CHART

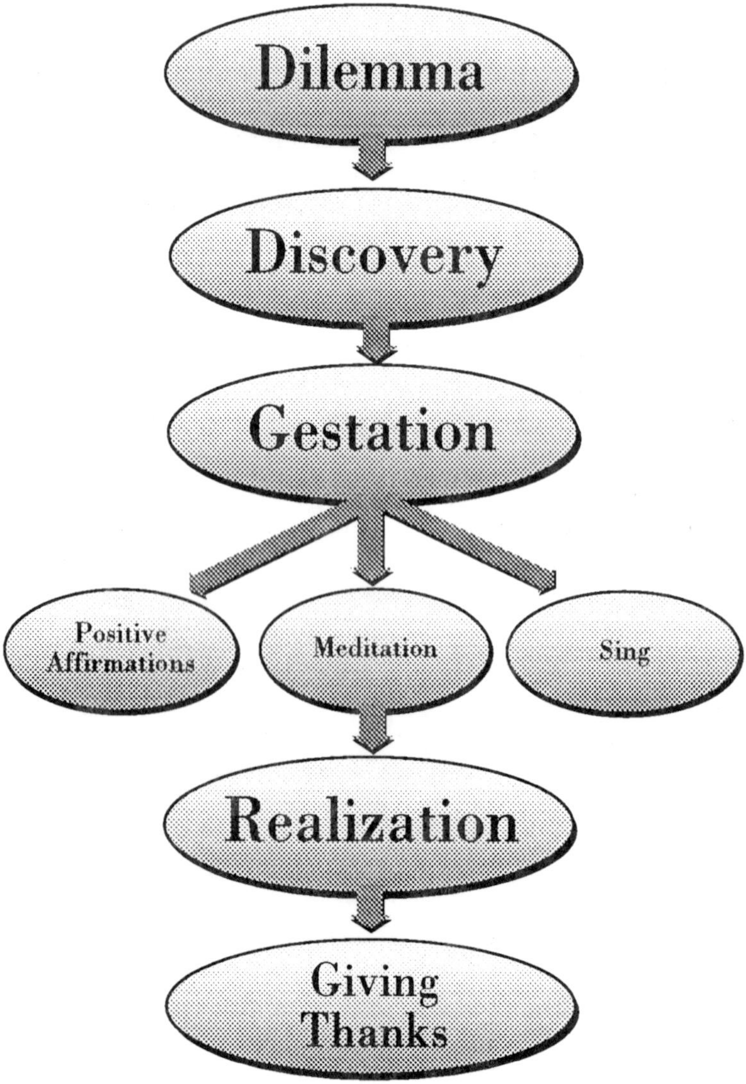

Based on the work of Alexander Everett

SECTION IX

CONCLUSION

STRATEGY 73

Your Personal "Growth Chart"

The following chapter and diagram on the opposite page are designed to help you in the decision-making processes that you encounter each day. When you have a major choice to make in your life, refer back to this section. Once it is ingrained in your way of thinking, you'll find that decisions are much easier to make, and that you'll work faster and more efficiently than ever before.

There are five steps to growth. It begins with the ***dilemma*** itself—we're all confused at one time or another. Wise people take this confusion and turn it into the second step: ***discovery***. This step gives us the opportunity to look for new answers and alternatives to a situation.

The third step is crucial. The ***gestation*** period is the time you devote to weighing your alternatives once you've decided exactly what they are. There are three different ways to engage in this process. The first is through positive affirmations; the second is through meditation; and the third is to change our mind's dominant thoughts to something else.

During this third step, the fourth will usually "magically" come about — ***realization*** will shed light on what we're asking for. Once you can accept this decision, the final process of ***giving thanks*** surfaces, the celebration manifests itself, and we can relax.

There are always choices. When one door closes, another opens — that's the way it's always been. **When you turn every mistake into an asset, your life will take a new direction — a very positive one!**

STRATEGY 74

Harnessing the Energy

Power comes from knowing how to do something. Knowledge springs from eyes that are always open and hands that are always working. If you look at human beings, the human spirit, we ARE energy. We happen to be here on planet Earth at this time to render our services *now.*

Change is a constant that we live with, grow with, and must learn to accept. Spirituality is that understanding which brings us control, and yet tells us that there is much more than we are currently achieving.

When we love our work, it shows. When we're dissatisfied, it can affect not only our professional lives, but our personal lives and the lives of those around us. If you limit yourself, you also limit the possibilities that might have been opened to you.

It's important to claim your own power, as so many leaders have done before us. Accept the challenges and growth that come with newfound opportunities.

In this book, I hope that I have stressed the importance of communication — not just with others, but with yourself. Inner and outer communication is essential to surviving in today's world. Take these skills you've learned and use them. Share them. These ideas are only as good as the person who uses them — use them to fulfill your destiny.

My parting advice to you is to work harmoniously today to build that better tomorrow.

Congratulations! This is the beginning!

CAREER SKILLS LIST

Based on the work of Paul Breen and Urban Whitaker

INFORMATION MANAGEMENT SKILLS:

ABILITY TO

1. prioritize responsibilities
2. define items by importance
3. collect data
4. analyze information
5. identify priorities
6. evaluate communications for effectiveness
7. combine facts and ideas for comprehensive program
8. define role of information and organize its relationship to project
9. execute recommendations from others regarding information
10. determine efficiency of data

DESIGN AND IMPLEMENTATION SKILLS:
ABILITY TO

1. develop alternative plans of action
2. establish realistic objectives
3. seek out more than the first right answer
4. create decisive plans
5. make future projections based on available data
6. incorporate "what if" scenarios
7. determine best choices of time, energy, and resource commitment
8. initiate and maintain accurate records
9. develop events/time schedule
10. avoid indecision or ambiguity

Research and Inquisitive Skills:

Ability To

1. synergize variety of information from many sources
2. test data using scientific method
3. use 4-way test of Rotary International®
   a. Is it truth?
   b. Is it fair to all concerned?
   c. Will it build goodwill and better friendships?
   d. Will it be beneficial to all concerned?
4. investigate challenges
5. clarify desires and goals
6. build plans that yield solutions
7. act in a non-judgmental fashion
8. listen fairly to alternative points of view
9. phrase answers to allow for formation of more choices
10. brainstorm with others for ideas

Communication Skills:
Ability To

1. listen and record objectively
2. clarify complicated ideas
3. strengthen interpersonal relations skills
4. improve group presentation skills
5. incorporate variety of media formats to project ideas
6. offer opinions without offending others
7. use specific and accurate details when describing events
8. be imaginative when evaluating other points of view
9. hone problem-solving abilities
10. radiate positive attitude inward and outward

Being Human:
Ability To

1. lead a team toward common objective
2. bond with others
3. create bridges from person to person, idea to idea
4. delegate responsibility
5. live in present time, not past experience or future expectations
6. work toward highest good and greatest joy
7. interface with others
8. communicate with others verbally and non-verbally
9. persuade others to achievement by setting examples
10. stand up for your beliefs
11. explore opportunities
12. take risks
13. accept responsibility
14. share skills, teach others
15. improve surroundings, community
16. develop ability to work under pressure

Non-judgmental Thinking Skills:

Ability to

1. cut through the clutter
2. identify priorities quickly and accurately
3. make solid decisions and suggestions
4. outline challenges
5. assess outside opinions
6. adopt and adapt to change
7. implement T-Graph (Truth Graph)
8. clarify thoughts through writing
9. determine strategies
10. bend rules or suspend judgment while looking at other points of view
11. map out alternative choices
12. brainstorm with others for solutions
13. evaluate potential answers
14. make recommendations

Management and Administration Skills:

Ability To

1. discover challenging tasks
2. explore new sources of ideas within organization
3. help others build self-confidence
4. praise others' work
5. encourage teamwork
6. promote general welfare of the universe
7. negotiate for better deals
8. re-direct responsibilities
9. stress individual importance and relationship to the whole
10. lead by example

Value-Added Skills:
Ability To

1. recognize that thought is creative
2. institute a course of action for improvement in working conditions
3. balance decisions that will lead to fulfillment of individual and group goals
4. determine value of arts, science, literature, and technology
5. choose to improve quality of life
6. look inward, seeking out one's own values
7. become one with inner self
8. free yourself from past experience
9. expect to succeed

Internal/Career Development Skills:

ABILITY TO

1. learn from life
2. transfer skills
3. build networks
4. balance achievements with expectations
5. instigate personal growth values
6. become aware of and use own strength
7. eliminate negative from thinking, from life
8. strive for excellence
9. be kind to yourself
10. develop persistence and patience
11. be open to change
12. generate trust and confidence
13. expect the unexpected
14. invest in yourself

GLOSSARY

Active Listening - openly demonstrating your interest to a potential client or employer by repeating their phrases back or echoing.

Boogles - worries, self-doubts that can plague average human beings at any time. Easily cured when recognized promptly.

Chain of Referral - starting with the local (or entry level) person to eventually reach the top dog.

Confidence - from the Latin "con fidelis" or "with Faith" — the only way to live a full life.

Desire - from the Latin "of the Father" — this is what is given to you from the Divine One. From there, YOU make it happen!

Destiny - the product of believing that all life is a leap of Faith — that all you have to do is ask and listen for the answers.

Dreamboard - collection of representations of an individual's dreams (magazine ads, newspaper pictures, family photos) to remind that person every day that those goals are achievable!

Echoing - the subtle technique of extending a conversation by rephrasing and repeating what's being said to you, or using a word like "oh?"

Energy - what we use to drive us through life — fueled by our mind-power and sustained by love (of life and of ourselves!)

Enthusiasm - from the Latin "enthos" meaning "the God-spirit within" — our inner drive

Evidence - concrete documents that attest to your capabilities and achievements. Often gathered and used in book form by successful people!

Faith - Father And I Together Here. You are never alone. We are all one.

Feel, Felt, Found - process of subtly turning a person's attitude toward your own — "Others feel as you do, and many have felt that way before, but what they've found is that..."

Ben Franklin T-Graph - diagram used to weigh both sides of an important decision. Having all the choices written out helps to determine which road is best.

Goal - a dream with a deadline.

Gold - what we make by recycling rejection. Turn the "no" into "I'll be happy to help you!"

Growth - what's attained through solving problems, and turning them into learning experiences that enrich your life.

Hidden Job Market - where 85 - 95% of all new jobs are found — those which do not come directly from ads in the classified section!

Invention - the result of a problem-solving search.

Kissing Cousins - Three questions that are closely linked, and most frequently used by interviewers: "Tell me a little about yourself," "What are your strengths?" and "Why could I hire you?"

Lumpy Mail - attention-getting direct mail piece that helps you to stand out from other employment candidates.

Mirror Work - using a mirror to discover whether you look confident when answering tough questions in an interview.

Networking - developing contacts through friends, volunteer projects, and job situations to look for opportunities to better yourself.

Passion - Burning desire — the inner drive to achieve a goal with any effort necessary.

Procrastination - fear-based problem of not dealing with reality or timeframes and deadlines set by yourself or others. 100% cure rate when properly treated!

Screen Test - given by the secretary to determine whether you're worthy of an appointment with the boss. Study hard, and you'll pass (through) with flying colors!

Transferable Skills - abilities being used in your present position which may lend themselves to other opportunities. These are usually not immediately recognized by the people who possess them, but they certainly exist!

Unique Selling Position - your outstanding qualities which set you apart from other candidates, and persuade employers to hire YOU!

Visualization - the process of actually picturing yourself in a given situation. Used as a form of boosting self-confidence to attain those goals.

Weakness Trap - the ploy of the interviewer who wants you to give him reasons not to hire you! Remember to combat this by turning weaknesses into positives!

INDEX

E

F

G

H

I

K

L

M

BIBLIOGRAPHY AND SUGGESTED READING

The Career Guide: Dun's Employment Opportunities Directory

Company Profile Resources Microfiche Collection

Encyclopedia of Associations

Standard and Poor's Register of Corporations, Directors, and Executives

Ward's Business Directory of US Private and Public Companies

Alessandra, Tony, Barrera, Rick and Weyler, Philip. *Non-Manipulative Selling*, Prentice-Hall, New York, NY - 1987

Bolles, Richard Nelson. *What Color Is Your Parachute?*, Berkley Books, New York - 1990

Boy Scouts of America. *Boy Scout Handbook* - 1988

Breen, Paul and Urban Whitaker. *Career Trasferrable Skills*- 1981

Burke, Jane and Lenore Yuen. *The Procrastination Cure Special Report*, Nightingale-Conant, Chicago, IL - 1990

Casale, Tony. *Tracking Tomorrow's Trends*, Listen & Learn USA, New York, NY - 1986

Dawson, Roger. *The Secrets of Power Negotiating*, Nightingale-Conant, Chicago, IL - 1987

Dictionary of Occupational Titles, Fourth Edition, US Department of Labor, Washington, DC - 1977

Dyer, Wayne. *The Awakened Life: Beyond Success, Achievement, and Performance,* Nightingale-Conant, Chicago, IL - 1987

Dyer, Wayne. *Gifts From EYKIS,* Simon & Schuster, Inc., New York, NY - 1983

Dyer, Wayne. *Transformation: You'll See It When You Believe It,* Nightingale-Conant, Chicago, IL - 1987

Dyer, Wayne. *Your Erroneous Zones,* Funk & Wagnalls, New York, NY - 1976

Falvey, Jack. *After College: the Business of Getting Jobs,* Williamson Publishing, Charlotte, VT - 1986

Falvey, Jack. *What's Next: Career Strategies After 35,* Williamson Publishing, Charlotte, VT - 1987

Firestien, Roger L. *Why Didn't I Think of That?,* United Educational Services, Inc., East Aurora, NY - 1989

Fisher, Roger. *Elements of Negotiation,* Tape Data Media, Inc., New York, NY - 1985

Gillies, Jerry. *Money Love: How To Get The Money You Deserve For Whatever You Want,* Warner Books, New York, NY - 1978

Goodman, Gary. *You Can Sell Anything By Telephone,* Prentice-Hall, New York, NY - 1984

Herman, Roger E. *The Process of Excelling,* Oakhill Press, Cleveland, Ohio - 1988

Haroldson, Mark. *How To Wake Up the Financial Genius Inside You,* Bantam Books, Salt Lake City, UT - 1976

Hill, Napoleon. *Think and Grow Rich,* Fawcett Crest, New York - 1960

Hopkins, Tom. *"How To Master The Art of Selling Anything,"* Sound Selling, Tom Hopkins International, Scotsdale, AZ - 1982

Jackson, Gerald. *Executive ESP: Shaping Prosperity and Review,* Simon & Schuster Sound Ideas, New York, NY - 1989

Jampolsky, Gerald. *Love Is Letting Go Of Fear: 12 Steps to Greater Happiness,* Nightingale-Conant, Chicago, IL - 1985

Johnson, Spencer, M.D. *The Quickest Way to Increase Your Prosperity,* Avon Books, New York, NY - 1984

Johnson, Spencer, M.D. and Larry Wilson. *One Minute Sales Person,* Avon Books, New York, NY - 1984

Johnson, Spencer, M.D. and Kenneth Blanchard. *The One Minute Manager,* Berkley Books, New York, NY - 1981, 1982

Johnson, Steve, Bob Rodgers, and Bill Alexander. *Secrets of the Hidden Job Market,* Betterway Publications, Inc., Whitehall, VA - 1986

Kessler, Rick and Linda Pollack. *Ad Facs 1990,* Ad Facs, Albany, NY - 1990

King, Charles M. *Overcoming the Overwhelming,* Oakhill Press, Cleveland, Ohio - 1991

King, Norman. *Big Sales From Small Spaces,* Facts or Files Publications, New York, NY - 1986

Knoll, Herbert Jr. *The Total Executive,* JELIA Publishing, Buffalo NY - 1985

Kojm, Christopher. *The ABCs of Defense: America's Military in the 1980s,* Editors of the Foreign Policy Association, Headline Series 254 - 1981

Korn, Lester. *The Success Profile,* Simon & Schuster, New York, NY - 1987

LeBoeuf, Michael. *Working Smarter,* Nightingale-Conant Corporation, Chicago, IL - 1987

Leeds, Dorothy. *PowerSpeak,* Prentice-Hall Press, New York, NY - 1988

Leeds, Dorothy. *Smart Questions,* Berkley Books/McGraw-Hill, New York, NY - 1988

Levinson, Jay Conrad. *Guerilla Marketing: Secrets for Making Big Profits From Your Small Business,* Houghton Miffin Co, Boston, MA - 1984

MacKay, Harvey. *Beware The Naked Man Who Offers You His Shirt,* Wm. Morrow & Co., New York, NY - 1990

MacKay, Harvey. *Swim With The Sharks Without Being Eaten Alive,* Wm. Morrow & Co., New York, NY - 1988

Maltz, Maxwell. *Psychocybernetics,* Simon & Schuster, New York, NY - 1960

Manning, Al G. *Help Yourself With ESP,* Parker Publishing Co, West Wyack, NY - 1964

Manning, Al G. *The Miraculous Laws of Universal Dynamics,* ESP Library, Edgewood, TX - 1981

McCormick, Mark. *What They Still Don't Tell You at Harvard Business School,* Bantam Audio, New York, NY - 1987

Molloy, John T. *Dress For Success,* Warner Books, New York, NY - 1975

Naisbett, John. *Megatrends,* Warner Books, New York, NY - 1984

Naisbett, John and Patricia Aburdne. *Megatrends 2000,* William Morrow and Company, New York, NY - 1990

Nelson, Robert B. *The Job Hunt,* Ten Speed Press, New York, NY - 1986

Nierenberg, Gerald I. *Nierenberg on Negotiating,* Success Motivation Cassettes, Inc., Waco, TX - 1983

Nightingale-Conant. *Sound Selling: The Audio Magazine for Sound Success,* Nightingale-Conant, Chicago, IL - 1990

Nightingale, Earl. *Lead The Field,* Nightingale-Conant, Chicago, IL - 1987

Occupational Outlook Handbook, US Department of Labor, Washington, DC - 1988-89

Ogilvy, David. *Ogilvy On Advertising,* Crown Publishers, New York, NY - 1983

Petras, Kathryn and Ross. *The Only Job Hunting Guide You'll Ever Need,* Poseidon Press, New York, NY - 1989

Ries, Al and Jack Trout. *Marketing Warfare,* New American Library - McGraw-Hill, New York, NY - 1986

Ries, Al and Jack Trout. *Positioning: The Battle For Your Mind,* McGraw-Hill, New York, NY - 1980

Robbins, Anthony. *Personal Power,* Robbins Research International, Irwindale, CA - 1989

Robbins, Anthony. *Unlimited Power,* Simon & Schuster Audio Publishing Division, New York, NY - 1986

Roger, John and Peter McWilliams. *You Can't Afford The Luxury of a Negative Thought,* Prelude Press, Los Angeles, CA - 1989

Ross, Marilyn and Tom. *The Complete Guide to Self-Publishing: Everything You Need To Know To Write, Publish, Promote, and Sell Your Own Book,* Writers' Digest Books, Cincinnati, OH - 1989

Ross, Marilyn and Tom. *Marketing Your Book,* Communication Creativity - 1989

Sabah, Joe and Judy. *How To Get The Job You Really Wanted and Get Employers To Call You,* Pacesetter Publications, Denver, CO - 1988

Sabah, Joe and Judy. *How To Get On Radio Talk Shows Without Leaving Your Home Or Office,* The Pacesetter Group, Denver, CO - 1988

Sackheim, Maxwell. *How To Advertise Yourself,* MacMillan Publishing Co, Inc., New York, NY - 1978

Schuller, Robert. *Be Happy You Are Loved,* Bantam Books, New York, NY - 1988

Schuller, Robert H. *Tough Times Never Last But Tough People Do!,* Bantam Books, New York, NY - 1984

Silva, Michael A. and R. Craig Hickman. *Creating Excellence,* Tape Date Media, Inc., New York, NY - 1985

Slutsky, Jeff. *Streetfighting: Low Cost Marketing,* Streetfighter Press, Columbus, Ohio - 1984

Stevenson, Regis J. *The Practical Psychology of Employment Interviewing,* Achievement Programs, Buffalo, NY - 1978

Townsend, Robert. *Further Up The Organizational Ladder,* Nightingale-Conant, Chicago, IL - 1989

Tracy, Brian. *Getting Rich in America,* Nightingale-Conant, Chicago, IL - 1989

Tracy, Brian. *The Psychology of Achievement,* Nightingale-Conant, Chicago, IL - 1986

Tracy, Brian. *The Psychology of Selling: The Art of Closing Sales,* Nightingale-Conant, Chicago, IL - 1985

VonOech, Roger. *A Whack On The Side of The Head,* Nightingale-Conant, Chicago, IL - 1987

Waitley, Denis and Thomas Budzynski. *The Subliminal Winner,* Nightingale-Conant, Chicago, IL - 1987

Walther, George. *Phone Power for Getting Appointments,* Nightingale-Conant, Chicago, IL - 1988

Watzlawick, Paul, John Weakland, and Robert Fisch. *Change Principles of Problem Formation and Problem Resolution,* W.W. Norton & Co, New York, NY - 1974

Wilde, Stuart. *The Force,* White Dove International, Inc., Taos, NM - 1987

Ziglar, Zig. *See You At The Top,* Nightingale-Conant, Chicago, IL - 1987

Over the period of many years during which research was done for this book, many notes were extracted from other publications. While the author made every attempt to give credit where it was due, he may have been unaware of the origin of each idea, and may have inadvertently failed to provide proper credit. The author sincerely regrets any omission and will correct the text if advised.

ORDER YOUR COPY

OF

THE CHANGING JOB JUNGLE

Send me _____ copies of *The Changing Job Jungle* at the special discount price of $11.95 per book. , plus $4.00 postage and handling for each book

Total enclosed $________

Please type or print:

Your Name ____

Address ____

City ______________________ State______ Zip__________

Phone Number ( ) ___________________________

Type of Business _____________________________________

Payment Method: ❑ **Check/Money Order**

❑ **VISA** ❑ **MasterCard**

Credit Card Exp. Date _________

Signature ____________________________________

Fold Here

Place
Stamp
Here

Kurt Barnaby Kojm, Senior Vice President
About-Face Executive Marketing
1833 Kensington Avenue
Buffalo, NY 14215

GIVE THE PERFECT GIFT

The Changing Job Jungle is the perfect gift — it gives your loved ones the opportunity to grow and achieve their dreams by using their own hidden talents! Whether it's a graduation, a birthday, or just an "I'm Thinking of You" present, you could be giving the recipient the chance of a lifetime!

All you need to do is fill out the order form below. We will mail the book first class, and enclose a personalized gift card. All books are autographed by the author!

Please enclose $11.95 plus $4.00 postage and handling for each book.

Please type or print:

Your Name ______________________________

Address ______________________________

City ________________ State ______ Zip __________

Phone Number (   ) ____________________

Please mail to:

Name ______________________________

Address ______________________________

City ________________ State ______ Zip __________

Phone Number (   ) ____________________

Inscription on gift card: ____________________

____

____

Payment Form:

❑ Check or Money Order Enclosed

❑ MC ❑ Visa # ______________________________

Expiration Date ______________________________

Cardholder's signature ____________________

Mail to: Kurt Barnaby Kojm, Senior Vice President
About-Face Executive Marketing
1833 Kensington Avenue
Buffalo, NY 14215

Fold Here

Place
Stamp
Here

Kurt Barnaby Kojm, Senior Vice President
About-Face Executive Marketing
1833 Kensington Avenue
Buffalo, NY 14215

Fold Here

Place
Stamp
Here

Kurt Barnaby Kojm, Senior Vice President
About-Face Executive Marketing
1833 Kensington Avenue
Buffalo, NY 14215